CLASSIC FILM SERIES

ONCE UPON A TIME IN AMERICA

2021 EDITION

by Chris Wade

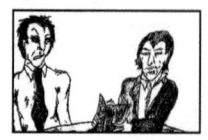

CLASSIC FILM SERIES:
ONCE UPON A TIME IN AMERICA
2021 EDITION
by Chris Wade

Wisdom Twins Books, 2021
wisdomtwinsbooks.weebly.com

This edition released in 2021

All rights reserved. No part of this publication may be reproduced, stored in a retrieval system, or transmitted in any form or by any means, electronic, mechanical, photocopy, recording or otherwise, without prior written permission of the copyright owner. Nor can it be circulated in any form of binding or cover other than that in which it is published and without similar condition including this condition being imposed on a subsequent purchaser.

ONCE UPON A TIME IN AMERICA

2021 EDITION

CONTENTS

Introduction

An Interview with James Woods

The Birth of A Classic

Themes and Subtext

Reaction and Legacy

References and Acknowledgements

About Chris Wade

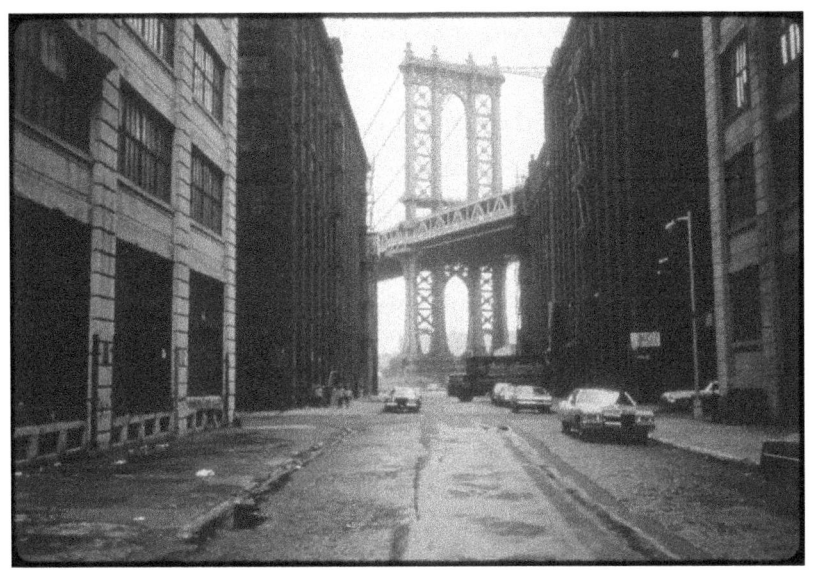

INTRODUCTION

When the subject of the modern gangster movie is brought up, the first films which come into most people's minds are undoubtedly The Godfather and GoodFellas. They are masterpieces of the highest degree, and they transcend the boundaries of the gangster genre. Yet as much as Coppola's grandiose epic trilogy and Scorsese's highly quotable glimpse into the mob encapsulate both the superficially finer and fundamentally ugly aspects of the gangster's life, there is one film which often gets put a little further down the list. It's a movie that hits the spot in terms of portraying the mobster's life and fate, albeit in a more poetic fashion. It's a slower, more careful piece of filmmaking, a meditation on reflection, the relativity of time, on loyalty and friendship. It is a film of ponderous, subtle beauty and unflinching bare truth - Sergio Leone's staggering epic, Once Upon a Time in America.

As strong an entry in the genre it is, in some ways it seems wrong to call Once Upon a Time in America a gangster film at all. Yes, the main characters happen to be gangsters (Jewish ones, as it happens, as opposed to the more common Italian-Americans), but they could just have easily been, say, shopkeepers, tailors or cops - if not for the killing of course. For fundamentally, the most violent moments aside, it's a film about strong bonds, time itself, memory and regret, a surrealistic cinema-dream that at once feels like both a hard punch in the stomach and a warm comforting blanket of hazy nostalgia. This dichotomy, this pull between brutality and beauty, is what makes the film so unique. In the hands of a lesser filmmaker the results might have jarred, but Leone, the master he was, turns a gangster picture about the weight of consequence and the power of loyalty into a mind bending odyssey through time itself.

Throughout the film, the gangsters, led by Robert De Niro as Noodles and James Woods as Max, perform unspeakable acts; thankfully for them, and for us, the film never asks for our admiration of these men. Paradoxically, though they do commit extremely vile acts on the screen, often unforgivably so, we still care how their collective tales pan out. Is this a credit to Leone's romanticised vision of the American outlaw, or is it mostly down to the performances, particularly the ones given by James Woods and Robert De Niro? The answer is both, and of course, much more.

Once Upon a Time in America is an epic on the grandest scale, into the creation of which hundreds of people contributed their all, ensuring the film affects and evokes consistently for its near four hour duration. But this monstrous, sweeping saga is told through characters, feelings and human interaction, not through mere visual extravagance alone. Yes, the sets and locations are stunning, and Leone handles them masterfully, but the emphasis is on relationships, fatal human flaws and personal complexities. Crime is secondary here, it's the people that count, and Leone, along with his dazzling cast (one of the best ever assembled I might add), work together to achieve the closest thing to perfection possible in the movies.

This book takes a look at the making of this classic film, exploring the subtext and themes running through it, while remaining primarily a celebration of a truly remarkable picture. It contains cast and crew recollections, who take us back in time to life on a Leone set and offer us a glimpse into the making of a masterpiece. This revised edition also features a brand new interview with James Woods, conducted by the author in December 2020. I was extremely honoured to speak to one of my film heroes, and he shared wonderful memories about a film that has always meant a lot to me. Personally, it has been an amazing experience putting together this little book, and I would be thrilled if readers thought any of my passion and enjoyment has made it onto the page.

I hope you enjoy the book.

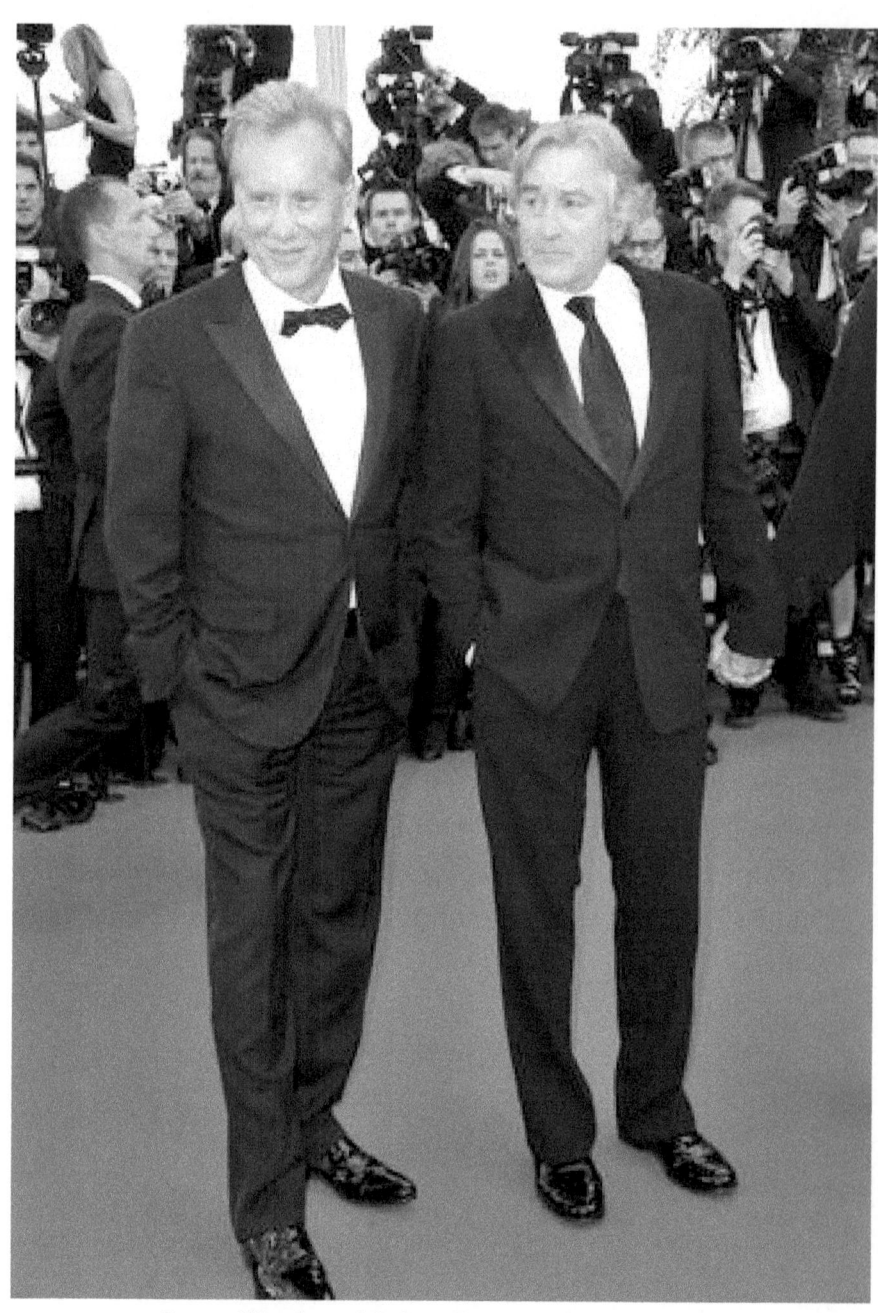

James Woods and Robert De Niro, Cannes, 2012

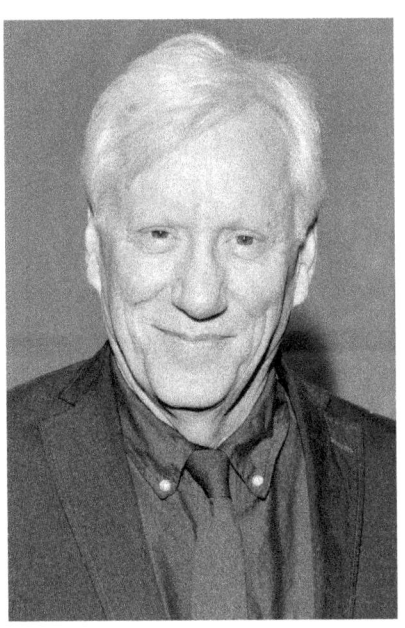

AN INTERVIEW WITH JAMES WOODS

*"Sergio Leone died of a broken heart because the savages of
Hollywood refused to recognise a Giant of Cinema."*
- James Woods to the author, 2020

As a huge fan of Once Upon a Time in America since my teens, naturally I am also a long time admirer of James Woods. Since the 1970s he has been one of America's leading character actors, a wild and exciting performer who brings every one of his roles to life in such a way that he almost redefines what film acting is. Think of his performances in such films as The Onion Field, David Cronenberg's Videodrome and Oliver Stone's Salvador; Woods reveals himself as an actor on the edge, a man in search of answers who may or may not get them before the movie's end. What I find remarkable about Woods is the fact he does not fall back on repeated mannerisms or go-to options. We know he gives his all to every role, but it also seems he comes up with new characteristics and gestures to suit each person. And looking at his parts over the years reveals his sheer range; the steely determination of lawyer Danny Davis in the brilliant Indictment: The McMartin Trial; the cold and ironically self destructive Max in Videodrome; the hopelessly ambitious but ultimately doomed Lenny in 1988's The Boost; the functioning but occasionally unpredictable criminal in Another Day in Paradise; the sleazy pimp Lester Diamond of Casino, complete with manipulative hand gestures, designed to keep Ginger where he wants her; the firm detective in 1988's seminal crime thriller, Cop. Every role is unique, and there aren't many actors you can say that about.

In Once Upon a Time in America, he is perfect as Max, at once both a carefully conniving businessman and a psychotic ready to explode at any time. It's a true tour de force. But he is a torn man, a character so much more complex than one might first believe.

I was pleasantly surprised when James Woods said he was happy to speak to me for this book, but his readiness should not have shocked me, given it's all about a film which means a lot to him. It is, to Woods, perhaps the finest film he has ever been in. I rang him from my home in Yorkshire on a rainy Sunday at 8 pm, a few days before Christmas. James Woods answered the phone in sunny Los Angeles at noon. From the word go he made it clear how much he loved the film, and his passion and pride for both Sergio Leone and Once Upon a Time in America was infectious. It was a wonderful conversation which my teenage self would not have deemed possible.

I didn't even need to begin with a question, because Woods started the ball rolling. "I'm so glad you called me," Woods began with warm enthusiasm. "I loved the movie; I loved all the people on it. I mean, it was a great personal experience. Some things you've done you're very proud of them, great movies, but they may have been difficult to do. Not that this (Once Upon a Time in America) wasn't difficult to do, it was definitely a challenge, but on others you just might not have had a personal best experience. You know, this was just a particularly joyous experience. All the people who were in it stayed friends for life, and we look back on it as a great moment in our lives. When I was at the anniversary screening of it at Cannes, I was with Bob and Jennifer Connolly and Elizabeth McGovern, and we were all on the red carpet... Gucci had spent over six million dollars on restoring the picture, Ennio Morricone was there, and I was with Bob and the reporters kind of noticed that De Niro was crying, he had tears in his eyes. I said 'Bob are you okay?' You know, I never really knew if Bob had liked the film a lot, because it was a little less realistic and a lot more operatic than the other stuff he had done on organised crime figures in the past; such legendary movies as Godfather Part II. And he said to me 'You know, this is the last time we'll ever do something like this.' I said 'What do you mean?' And he said 'Well...' I mean Bob is not a big publicity guy, he's very shy. He said 'You know, the red carpet for a film that's really great.' I asked him if he was going to watch the movie. He said 'Yeah, let's stay and watch it.' So we stayed and we watched it, and it was the full three hour forty two minute cut, which was shown at the Cannes Film Festival the night it first opened, where it got, I'm not kidding, a twenty minute standing ovation. It was stunning, *stunning*."

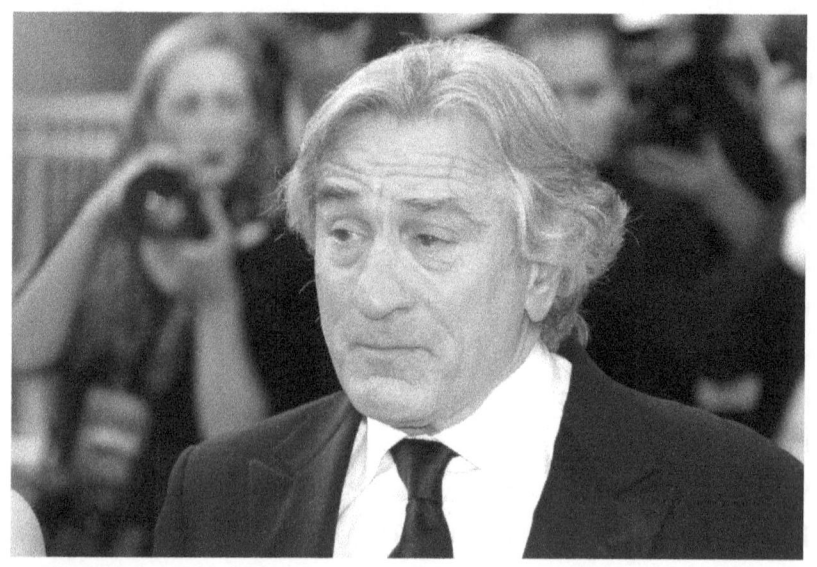

Robert De Niro, clearly moved at the Cannes screening, 2012

James then described his reaction at seeing the full cut again, all those years later. "It started deliberately... I won't say slowly, but deliberately, with the music. And I thought 'Oh my God, when this movie is seen the way it was supposed to be seen...' It just lulled you into this other world, this opium dream really, that was so mesmerising. I mean, the musical score, for my money, is perhaps the best musical score ever written for any movie. I just think that music is beyond anything I have ever heard. Ennio was sitting behind us and I turned and said 'Maestro', and he nodded and said 'Maestro' back, which I thought was really sweet."

On the subject of the score, James remembered: "When we did the final scene with Bob and myself... Secretary Bailey knows his days - well his *hours* - are numbered, and there was a scene - of course that the studio originally cut out as they did with everything else -

between me and Treat Williams' character, the head of the trucker's union. You see what the problem is; it's all defined in that scene. And then it comes to the final showdown scene and Bob comes in and denies recognising me, which is the cruellest thing he can do, after the cruelty I have perpetrated on him to save his life. Sergio said to me, 'Jimmy'..."

Woods paused and continued: "Let me just say I loved Sergio, I loved him, loved him, loved him. He was the greatest director, and he loved actors. Most directors are kind of afraid of actors or don't like them. Sergio loved his actors. He said 'Jimmy, I got a surprise for you.' I said 'What?' He said 'While we were shooting, I had Ennio go to London with the London Philharmonic to record the music for this scene.' I said 'Oh great, I'd love to hear it sometime.' He said 'No, I'm gonna play it during the scene.' So when we were shooting the scene, the master, we did it to the music playing all over the set. I mean, it's one thing to see a movie, the scene with the music playing, but when you are doing a scene and acting to it, and Ennio Morricone's music is playing! I mean, we had to re-do our vocal sounds for that, and it was covered in the close ups. But I can't explain to you the chills that Bob and I both felt. It was amazing, just an amazing experience. I think that's why that scene - which many people think is one of Sergio's best scenes from his movies - was so good because the gravitas of that scene was imparted to all of us by the playing of that beautiful music through the actual filming. A great experience."

I said to James that it is difficult to imagine the film without that wonderful music, given it adds power to every moment it is played over. "Well, not only the moment," James said, "but it defines the film. You have to remember, in Once Upon a Time in America, there is a moral stress and dynamic struggle for balance for each character. Each character is trying to do a good thing in the process of doing bad things. My betrayal of my guys, and I sacrifice Cockeye and Patsy, to save Bob, to save Noodles... I am still trying to save his life. Casting him into anonymity for the rest of his life, going to bed early in Buffalo..."

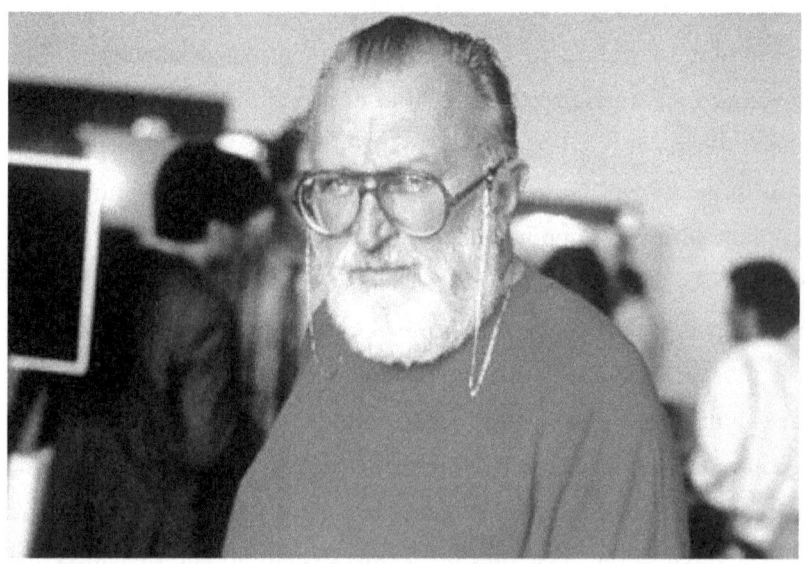

Sergio Leone, 1980s

I found it interesting when James mentioned the word balance because I have always seen Once Upon a Time in America as a film about the balance between right and wrong. Much of the dynamic, and indeed the balance, comes in the performances of Woods and De Niro. I mentioned to James that the collaboration between him and De Niro often feels like one performance, and it is these two men and how they are portrayed by the two iconic actors, that give the film its edge and its tension. "Yes I believe that," Woods said, "and I have to say that Bob is an incredibly generous actor. And so were the other actors too, they were just a great bunch of people. Everybody has their balance; Deborah does, being in love with one man; the other man is powerful, and she wants to get away from the stench of the place, which she feels Noodles will always have. She has her balance. Certainly, Tuesday Weld's character (Carol), she goes from being married to being my mistress. They each have their own dynamic pull, and that triangle of Noodles, Max and Deborah is a very strong ménage of moral quandary."

James then explained what it really meant to collaborate with Robert De Niro, already America's most respected film actor.

"You have to remember too, that when we were making Once Upon a Time in America, Bob had just come off Raging Bull, one of the greatest performances ever put to film. And I was a virtual unknown. But I was playing a character where I was actually the strong and more ruthless of the two of us. So I not only had to be equal to Bob, to go toe to toe with him, I had to have the courage and confidence as a character and frankly as an actor, to be able to stand up and throw my punches against the greatest. I have to say that Sergio gave me that confidence. He felt that I was on to something; he loved my character and was very encouraging of my performance. And Bob was wonderful about letting me go headstrong into it. And I actually went against some of Bob's ideas. I remember we were doing the hospital scene, and I just kept staring at Bob all the time. And Bob said 'You know, maybe you shouldn't look at me all the time.' I think he was afraid that one actor was too concerned with another. But I knew that Max was preparing this catastrophe that was coming, and that I was in a sense almost longing to connect with him, to tell him even though I couldn't; that the only way I could save him was by sacrificing any love or trust we had had all our lives. The greatest tragedy is that in the end that love is denied to Max by Noodles, by doing the strongest and strangest thing possible; literally, to ignore his existence. So it was like a contest between a mongoose and a cobra, constantly snapping and dodging each other. It felt that way in every scene. And Bob and I became very good friends. I love Bob. We hung out a lot which was something I was very pleased about. We ended up spending time together. Yet when we worked, the dynamic went right back to that sparring dance that those two characters had. As we tried to explore our own characters, we found ourselves exploring each other's characters as well.

"A perfect example," Woods continued, "was when we were all supposed to laugh when I kicked Tuesday Weld out of the room, when I'm sat in the throne that I've bought. We rehearsed that for ten hours, and Bob said it was just corny, like those old guy movies where everyone laughs. He said 'We're not gonna break into laughter. It's corny and I don't think it works.' And he came up with the idea of stirring the cup, building the tension. We all liked that. He knows he's getting to me, as Max, and I know I am pressuring him by sitting in that throne with a cigar. Finally - and this was unusual because he's Bob De Niro, the leader, just phenomenal - Sergio said we were gonna have to come back tomorrow, because we hadn't shot anything. And I said 'Let's just shoot one!' And Bob said 'No', and I said 'Come on, we're gonna shoot one!' I kind of pushed it, sort of like going on to the end of the gang plank, and I took the chance that he would just go with one take to see what happened. And in that take, as in the script, I kicked her in the butt - very degrading to women, but that's what those guys did in that era - and I ad-libbed: 'Do I have a way with women or what?' And for some reason, because we were all so tired, we genuinely howled with laughter. We were exhausted. But it was because it was so unusual and quirky... And you must remember this was a huge monster movie costing tens of millions of dollars, one of the most expensive movies ever made. But it took that kind of improvisational levity to crack the scene and make it work, and then we were fine. Once we knew that laughter had happened legitimately, then it was OK, then we could do whatever.

"Bob was great, because he was always open to other actor's ideas. And he could never do anything false; it's not in his nature as an actor. He has a very difficult time doing anything unless it feels authentic - as do I, and all those wonderful actors in that film. We all felt we knew we were stepping up to the plate with the big hitter of life. You gonna work with Bob De Niro, you gotta be on your A-plus game in every minute. 'I'm working with a legend here, I'm gonna try and do a legendary performance within my own realm of ability or aspiration.' Not in a competitive way, but in a co-operative way, meaning that he is inspiring all of us; he is our muse to be our very best, and you hope that when you walk away thirty years from now, you'll say to people 'That was my greatest performance because I was inspired working with a giant.' And I dug as deep as I could to give him what he deserved. I always say if you like my performance, then know it was a homage to my brilliant acting partner and friend, Bob De Niro."

I also asked James about Sergio's looseness with the young actors on Once Upon a Time in America. On past films he admitted he had been stricter with his performers, but Woods, De Niro and the others showed him a new way of doing scenes. "To clarify that," Woods said, "What Sergio actually said was 'Jimmy, they say I'm an operatic director, where everything is staged because I am doing movement from a camera, so it's very precise. Now you and Bob have your own ideas about your characters, and it changes the movement and I've never worked like that. But I'm loving doing it because I can combine it with my way of working, and the two together give it an authenticity it's never had before.' He said: 'This is the first time I've worked with live sound.' And we had to get used to telling the crew to not talk during a scene, because they weren't used to live sound in Italy at that time. And what happened was, we would improvise small changes within scenes, but quite frankly the script was so tight that we didn't have to do a lot. But it was in the way that we moved. There's a lot of physical interaction between Bob and me in the film, in the sense that we got up really close to each other. Like in the scene when he calls me crazy. I wanted to have a sense that I was the cobra that could strike at any moment, because I was coiled up. My ambition and my greed were so powerful that I was coiled up a lot. And he was the guy who tried to make the wiser decision, and be careful not to go over the edge and put ourselves in a position where we could be destroyed. It was a tango between the two of us. Really quite frankly - I think you said it very well - two halves of the same man... Like the mythological character Janus, the two faces of this one struggling persona. They are all gangsters, they do what they have to do, but there is a high moral paradigm that they follow that is a matter of life and death for them. You got to be able to trust your brother, because that is what they were like, they were like brothers."

Me and James also talked about Max's paradox with Noodles; he loves him but he can't stop himself from destroying him in the process. I mentioned to James that I noticed a secret longing in Max, especially during scenes when he places his hand on Noodles, when he is up close and smiles at him; for after each warm smile, the smile is quickly erased and replaced by a look of sadness, of longing. "You know what?" James said. "I did that on purpose. No one has ever noticed it in all these years."

It is ultimately a tragedy, a love tale between two "brothers" torn apart by greed, competitiveness and the world which they have chosen as their environment. Both men, especially Noodles (as Deborah herself says) could have gotten away from the crime world; they could have walked away with their million in savings after the end of prohibition and taken it easy ("I'll take it easy when we have twenty million," Max hisses) but instead Max pushes it towards self destruction. "Redemption," James told me, "is out of grasp."

One part of the film which fans discuss and dissect is the ending. Is it Max/Bailey who goes into the back of the garbage truck? Though James has been asked about this millions of times, I could not resist. "Sergio had a photo double of me on set," James said. "You can't tell if it's me or not when Noodles looks back. Sergio wanted it that way. We want Bob to not be certain. To my knowledge I'm the only person Sergio ever explained the ending to. When I asked him why he used the photo double purposely, he said he wanted the audience and Noodles to be somewhat confused. I said to him that it obviously worked because I indeed was also confused. When I asked him point-blank if it was my character, Max (now Secretary Bailey) who jumped or was pushed into the garbage truck to his certain death, Sergio's exact words were, 'It's like Jimmy Hoffa. You don't know, but you know!' The Hoffa reference is a very important part of American organized crime urban legend. For decades people have speculated about the truth of how he was kidnapped and murdered, right up to the making of The Irishman by Martin Scorsese, one of Sergio Leone's greatest admirers."

When Once Upon a Time in America was released in the United States, it was cut down to two hours and twenty minutes, and its events placed in chronological order. As a result, this sweeping, beautiful masterpiece was reduced to a routine crime story. It was one of the cruellest mistreatments in film history. James said that during an American preview screening, one audience member shouted out "Answer the damn phone!" during the opening sequence, when Noodles is haunted by the ringing of the phone call which altered the course of his whole life. Right from the word go, it was understood that American audiences would not get - nor would they wish to get - what Sergio's original version of the film was all about. Ludicrous changes were made from beginning to end, and whole scenes were cut, meaning that later sequences made no sense. When Noodles leaves Bailey's mansion, they even added a gun shot sound effect, just to hammer home the point that, yes, Max was dead. There was no room for ambiguity. They had mercilessly butchered a classic.

One final thought James had when speaking to me, was that Sergio was crushed by America's treatment of his beloved masterpiece. He boldly and beautifully declared: "Sergio Leone died of a broken heart because the savages of Hollywood refused to recognise a giant of cinema." James said this twice, repeated it with more feeling, and I made the point of writing it down in capitals. It seemed like the most important statement he could have come out with when discussing one of the greatest motion pictures in history.

I went away after talking to James moved by his love for the film, and also for Leone the man and the artist. Never have I heard an actor speak so proudly, so dearly, of something he has been a part of. And that is a tribute to both Once Upon a Time in America and the man who created it.

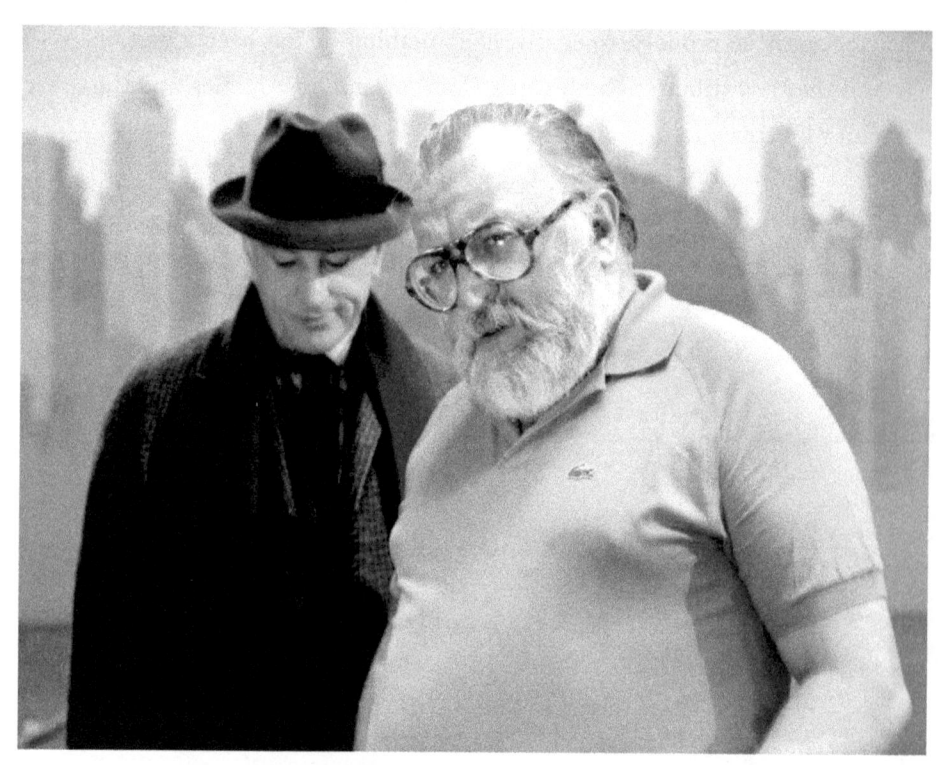

Robert De Niro and Sergio Leone during the filming of
Once Upon a Time in America

THE BIRTH OF A CLASSIC

All cinematic masterpieces start their life somewhere, and for Sergio Leone, the adventure began with a book he had read and fallen in love with in the 1960s, Hoods by Harry Grey. Leone loved Grey's inside take on the life of the Jewish mob, and was desperate to meet him. But Grey, real name Harry Goldberg, proved elusive for some time. Sergio knew he was the only man who could bring his story to life, and use Grey's tale as an allegory for the rise and fall of America; its prospering in the post-depression/pre-war period, then what some see as its moral and aesthetic decay in the 1960s.

For years the picture was an obsession to Leone, the "dream project" as others have referred to it. For a long time the film seemed an impossibility. In time though, once he began committing all of his energy and passion into bringing Hoods to the big screen, things he could never have imagined began to come to fruition.

Of course, Sergio was already an acclaimed filmmaker by then, and though his filmography was slim, most of his films had made a huge impact. Born in 1929 in Rome, he was the son of silent film actress Edvige Valcarenghi and influential film figure Roberto Roberti, born Vincenzo Leone in 1879. A prolific actor and famed director, his father made a string of films, most of which were silent, though he did direct a few in the sound era. By the time his old man died in 1959, Sergio had already set his sights on following in his father's foot steps and becoming a filmmaker. "My mother was an actress," Sergio told Marlaine Glicksman. "My father was an actor and a director. I am the son of filmmakers. I was born with this bow tie made of celluloid on my collar."

The young Sergio left school at 18 and began his career as assistant to Vittorio de Sica on the legendary Italian neorealist classic, The Bicycle Thief (1948). Leone also gained valuable experience as assistant director on seminal pictures like Ben Hur and Quo Vadis. Becoming a seasoned screenwriter through the early 1960s, he made his directorial debut in 1961 with The Colossus of Rhodes, a lavish Roman epic.

Though his first film turned a profit, it was in the western where Leone rose to prominence, the genre he is now most associated with. But using the western setting didn't necessarily make his films standard genre fare. Indeed, they were a world apart from the macho but loveable films of John Wayne. They were more ambiguous and mythical.

In Leone's Dollars Trilogy, Clint Eastwood starred as the enigmatic Man with No Name, a mysterious figure who said little because he didn't need to; his actions did the talking for him. Filmed in Spain, the films have perhaps become the most iconic and celebrated westerns of all time. Grouping together the stunning visuals, larger than life performances and marvellous Ennio Morricone musical scores, the films are still highly watchable to this day. Though plainly they are westerns in most aesthetic and stylistic concerns, Leone's messages ran deeper than the good versus bad story lines.

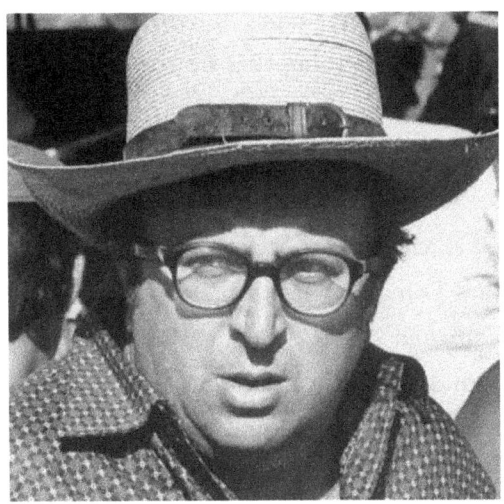
Sergio Leone in 1975

"I had never thought of making a western even as I was making it," Sergio said. "I think that my films are westerns only in their exterior aspects. Within them are some of my truths, which happily, I see, belong to lots of parts of the world. Not just America. My discussion is one that has gone all the way from Fistful of Dollars through Once Upon a Time in America. But if you look closely at all these films, you find in them the same meanings, the same humour, the same point of view, and, also, the same pains. I have to be honest about one thing. When I went to America, no one asked me how I was. Everyone always asked me, 'How much do you make?' But, of course, this happens in other parts of the world, and not just in America. But in America, it is particularly sure that you'll hear this question asked. Therefore, I consciously chose a person like the bounty killer [of the Fistful trilogy] because he was the street sweeper of the desert, a man who put his life at risk exclusively for the money. I'm not saying that he went against the law, but he put himself within the wings of the law only when it was something that he could profit by. Of course, there was also the myth of the western films. But my films are borrowed not from the story of the West in America but from the story of cinema. So it is clear that the vehicle of the western was a very interesting vehicle for me to contraband some of my ideas."

With his Dollars Trilogy under his belt (A Fistful of Dollars, For A Few Dollars More and The Good, the Bad and the Ugly), Leone looked onwards and upwards towards his new artistic ambition, the fabled "Once Upon A Time" Trilogy. The first instalment was made in 1968, the legendary and vividly violent Once Upon A Time in the West, starring Henry Fonda and Charles Bronson. Again, Leone reinvented the genre and brought it into the late sixties, its brutality pairing the film with the atrocities being acted out in Vietnam. These were violent times indeed, and Leone mirrored them on the screen.

Leone was then working as a producer on the 1971 film Duck You Sucker for director Peter Bogdanovich, but when the young buck and the old pro began to disagree on artistic grounds, Leone took over as director. Also known as A Fistful of Dynamite and Once Upon A Time... the Revolution, the film was the second part in Leone's trio of American themed tributes. The third entry, which would take over a decade to see a serious development, was still some way away.

In 1971, Leone famously turned down the chance to direct the movie adaptation of Mario Puzo's hot novel, The Godfather, quite simply because there was a crime story of his own he wanted to see make it to the big screen. The Hoods, though not a massively well known book, spanned the 20s and 30s, and took the reader - in this case a wild eyed and excited Sergio Leone - inside the world of a group of gangsters. By focusing on the Jewish mob, right away the film was separated from The Godfather and other Italian-American themed gangster flicks. Therefore it was harder to get financing.

To Leone, this was it, the one film he really wanted to make. Between the release of Duck You Sucker and the eventual surfacing of Once Upon A Time in America in 1984, Leone was also attached to two other projects - My Name is Nobody as uncredited director, and A Genius, Two Partners and a Dupe, as co-director. But these projects were merely filling time while his fantasy film was being developed.

In his interview with Marlaine Glicksman, Leone spoke of his decision to wait for the right film, rather than just slog through commission jobs as other filmmakers were prone to do. "Producing films was a distraction for me for which I paid dearly," he said. "Because I realized than an author cannot also be a producer. Therefore, I had more trouble than I had a sense of utility or satisfaction. But it served to occupy me and to keep me occupied in a field that I love - which was cinema - while I was waiting to realize the film that I wanted to do, which was Once Upon a Time in America, which took ten years of thinking and working to realize. There are directors, and there are authors. I think I am more of an author than a director. I've tried to consider stories that I have read, making them into films, but they would turn out unnatural. If a producer wants that, he should call other people. Not me."

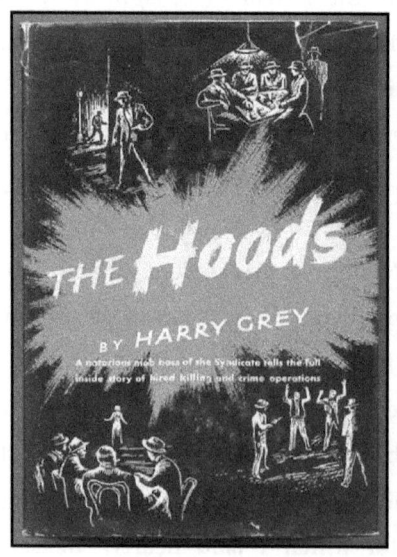 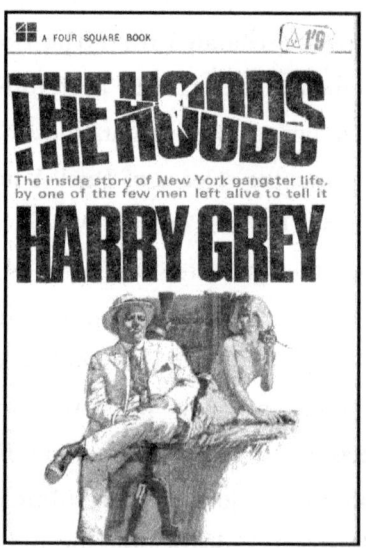

*Two editions of Harry Grey's novel The Hoods,
the inspiration for Leone's film.*

In essence, though he was using a gangster's memoir as the basis, Once Upon A Time in America was not only a love letter to America, however corrupt and rotten aspects of it were (and to some still are), but to classic American cinema. A man "fascinated with all films" as a young boy, this was his chance to make the ultimate homage to the classic gangster movies of the 1930s, the era of James Cagney and Edward G Robinson. Enchanted, Leone saw his adaptation of Hoods as a "loving hymn to the cinema." For Leone, Once Upon A Time in America quickly became an obsession. Upon the film's release, he would say to American Film Magazine that "the story of these Jewish gangsters—unlucky three times over and determined five times over to challenge the gods—attached itself to me like the malediction of the Mummy in the old movie with Boris Karloff. I wanted to make that film and no other."

Securing the rights to the book was a difficult task however. Leone contacted Harry Grey's literary agent, saying "I would like to have a conversation with the man who wrote this book. If I buy the film rights to The Hoods it will not be a straightforward adaptation. I must have several discussions with the man who wrote it. I want to meet the man who calls himself Harry Grey!"

But Harry wasn't interested, and turned down repeated requests for this famed filmmaker to meet him. And then, one day, just when Leone thought there was no hope, about to return to Italy fed up and disenchanted with the film industry, the telephone rang in his New York hotel. It was Harry Grey himself. Perhaps in the gap between the call and his last snub, Grey had done some research on Leone. The ice broke when Grey claimed to have enjoyed all of his Dollars movies. Seemingly now entrusting of the man in the director's chair, the pair had a good talk on the line before meeting up, with Leone's brother in law acting as interpreter. Leone was ecstatic. After all, he had just spoken to the real-life Noodles himself.

The pair met in a seedy bar, which Leone found perfectly fitting (the man serving them even looked like Fat Moe, the portly and likeable barman in Once Upon A Time in America), taking a window seat as Leone observed that Grey now resembled Edward G Robinson, even though he must have been over seventy by then. The "chat" proved to be mostly one sided. Leone and his brother in law could barely get more than a few words out of Grey. He agreed that he would act as consultant, yet apparently didn't seem excited about very much at all. But he was involved, and that was important.

Officially now, Leone had the author of the book on his side. Meeting the elder Harry had been an eye opening and illuminating experience too, in part inspiring Leone's decision to have Noodles as an older gentleman in the 1960s, looking back on his youth and those days as a rich and successful criminal. Had he not tracked down and met the real life Noodles, the film might have turned out much more conventional, and it has to be said, maybe less interesting too. Had he not managed to pin down the enigmatic, elusive Grey, Leone might not have even made it!

Leone later said that Grey had told him that he never imagined his story could be a film, and that he wrote The Hoods "against Hollywood, while he was imprisoned in Sing Sing. But, on the contrary, his book resembled a voice-over by a bad Hollywood screenwriter."

Even with Harry on board, getting the movie off the ground proved to be more difficult than Leone had imagined. "We began to procure rights to the cinematographic adaptation, which, however, was already in the hands of other film-world hombres," he told American Film. "It wasn't very easy, but we finally managed, with cleverness and many dollars, to rip off the rights from the legitimate holders. That was already the first sign of where things were heading. Then the infernal screenplay-writing season began. Norman Mailer was among the first to work on it. He barricaded himself in a Rome hotel room with a box of cigars, his typewriter, and a bottle of whiskey. But, I'm sorry to say, he only gave birth to a Mickey Mouse version. Mailer, at least to my eyes, the eyes of an old fan, is not a writer for movies."

Each screenplay draft which surfaced proved unsatisfactory to Leone, and failed to match his grand vision. It was the appearance of the young producer Arnon Milchan then, which began to change things around. The Israeli businessman had entered the film industry in the late 1970s, and had worked on a few films before meeting up with Sergio. Intent on backing the film, Milchan saw being attached to a Leone masterpiece as something of a coup, an honour in fact, and the pair enjoyed a healthy relationship. Arnon ensured that attention was given to Leone's view of what the finished picture should be, meaning he apparently had artistic control. The Ladd Company put up a large chunk of the money, and also signed up to the task of distributing Leone's film in the US via Warner Brothers.

Before this though, Leone had gone through a huge list of possible actors to play Noodles. The casting was vital, perhaps the most important decision to be made in the movie. In the early days of development, rather ironically, the role was sitting firmly in the lap of acclaimed French actor Gerard Depardieu. This was in 1975, around the time the film's eventual star, Robert De Niro, was filming with Depardieu in Italy for Bernardo Bertolucci's controversial epic, 1900. Gerard spoke little English at the time, and wanted the role so badly that he promised to learn English and attempt to perfect a convincing Brooklyn accent. However, for better or worse, this was not to be. (Other reports say he was set to play Max.) At the turn of the 1980s, Leone envisioned Paul Newman as the older Noodles and Tom Berenger as the younger man, and other names included James Cagney and Richard Dreyfus. For the role of Max, Noodles' best friend turned nemesis, Harvey Keitel and Dustin Hoffman were considered.

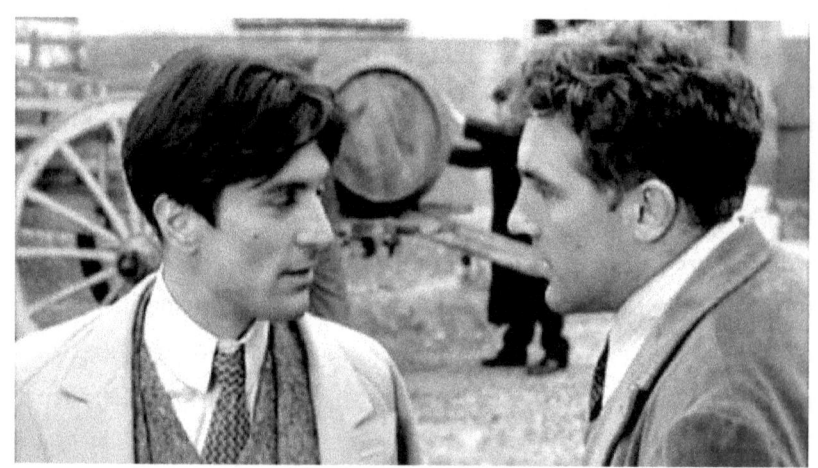

Robert De Niro in Bertolucci's Novicento (1976), with Gerard Depardieu, who was originally in line to play Noodles

Robert De Niro had been interested in the project for some time, and though Sergio saw countless performers, De Niro was incomparable. "I did six months of casting the film," Leone recalled, "I saw so many great actors. I was embarrassed when I finally had to make a choice. I find great spontaneity in American performers - no one is better than De Niro at being studied and spontaneous at the same time."

The reports about De Niro getting involved and committing to the film are interesting. Back in 1973, Leone had met up with Robert and a translator, outlining the project. De Niro, fresh off Mean Streets, hadn't familiarised himself with Leone and his work, and seeing as the two could not communicate directly due to language barriers, he put it down as a maybe, rather than a certified yes. "I liked Sergio," De Niro later said, "but I wasn't sure about him as a director. I knew he'd done spaghetti westerns but they weren't taken seriously - I certainly hadn't seen any of them."

It wasn't until years later that De Niro and Arnon Milchan met up with Sergio in his New York hotel that Robert signed up. At that point, the leading man with whom Leone was most associated with was, without question, Clint Eastwood, who had burned himself into the world's collective film going psyche with intensity in the Dollars Trilogy. A totally different beast to De Niro, even Leone himself couldn't help but note the vast juxtapositions between the two mega stars and their acting styles. In 1984 he observed, "It's difficult to compare Eastwood and De Niro. The first is a mask of wax. In reality, if you think about it, they don't even belong to the same profession. Robert De Niro throws himself into this or that role, putting on a personality the way someone else might put on his coat, naturally and with elegance, while Clint Eastwood throws himself into a suit of armour and lowers the visor with a rusty clang. It's exactly that lowered visor which composes his character. And that creaky clang it makes as it snaps down, dry as a martini in Harry's Bar in Venice, is also his character. Look at him carefully. Eastwood moves like a sleepwalker between explosions and hails of bullets, and he is always the same—a block of marble. Bobby, first of all, is an actor. Clint, first of all, is a star. Bobby suffers, Clint yawns..."

The script was finalised in October of 1981, and in the end it was credited to six men - Leone, Piero De Bernardi, Enrico Medioli, Franco Arcalli, Leonardo Benvenuti and Franco Ferrini. Anyone interested in the idea of a screenplay as a stand alone piece of work, rather than just a bare-boned blueprint for a film, should read the script to Once Upon A Time in America from front to back. Novelistic, expressive and highly detailed, it's a complex, mammoth and demanding read, but one that is almost as powerful as the finished film itself. (Note: The screenplay can be read online on various websites.) At 317 pages, the huge text (probably three times the length of an average film script at that time) was slaved away at for months, though there were delays along the way due to a three month long writer's strike in 1981.

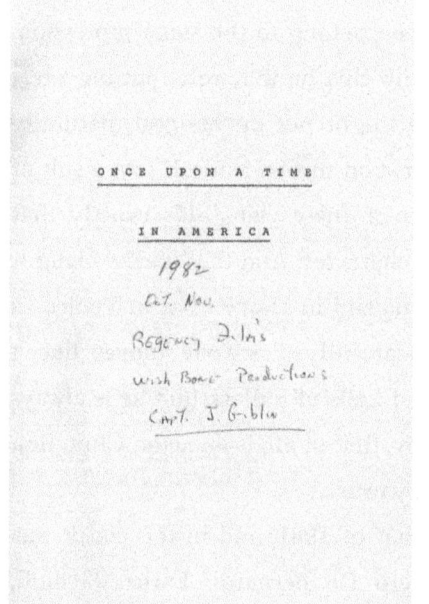

A 1982 draft of the script

Unusually, the script is divided into two columns. Down one side is a detailed description of what's going on sound-wise, like dialogue and even sound effects. On the other side is what's happening (or going to be happening) visually. Leone also opts for details on the time setting, which in the case of this film was essential.

For example:

SCENE 1 – SHADOW PUPPET THEATER. (1933) Interior. Night.

SCENE 2 – NOODLES' HOTEL ROOM. (1933) Interior. Night.

SCENE 3 – SHADOW PUPPET THEATER. (1933) Interior. Night. [again]

SCENE 4 – OFFICE AT FAT MOE'S SPEAKEASY. (1933) Interior. Night.

It also needs noting that there are scenes in the screenplay that aren't in the actual film. For example, scene 26 is set in a synagogue in 1968, and though it may just have been filmed, it hasn't been put into any released cut. The same goes for another earlier scene. As written in one draft, Noodles doesn't get the train to Buffalo, but hitchhikes and gets inside a truck. The driver asks him where he's going, and Noodles replies: "Where you're going." It is intriguing how the picture might have turned out had Leone filmed it this way.

Once Leone had the green light, he tried to get in touch with Harry Grey to tell him the good news. Grey's wife answered the phone and informed Sergio, sadly, that Grey had died several years earlier. Alas, he didn't live to see his book come to life on the screen; though it's hard to say if he would have cared either way.

Filming eventually began in June of 1982, and did not finish until April of the following year. Though Leone first attempted to merely produce while a younger filmmaker took on directing duties (John

Millius was on the cards to direct but signed up for another project instead), thankfully this plan was scrapped and he ended up in the director's chair himself. To have the film being directed (or should that be conducted perhaps?) by anyone else is unimaginable today, and given it was Leone's dream project, it would also have made little sense to pass over directorial duties to another. Given the fact that Leone had every single shot and scene mapped out in his head, it was essential that he be given room to breathe in order for the film to come to life on his terms. Given his track record, Leone knew about cinema, atmosphere and emotion, and even the studio men knew to stay clear and let him guide the way.

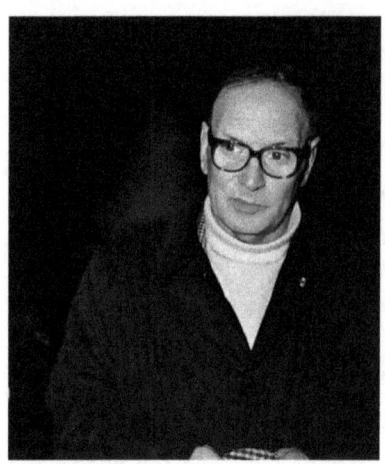

Ennio Morricone, the legendary composer, who scored Once Upon a Time in America

One area where the film was bound to excel was in the soundtrack. Leone's skill at combining visuals and music was so revered that even the great master Stanley Kubrick once rang him up to ask how he achieved a specific effect with music and pictures in Once Upon A Time in the West. The Ennio Morricone score and the Leone look were an inseparable celluloid duo, and on Once Upon A Time in

America their union would reach its peak in my view. Some of the music for the movie had already been recorded before filming, so Leone would play it on set to enhance the atmosphere. It created a wistful, sad and often longing feel, enhancing the emotions between the actors. One can imagine how breathtaking it sounded.

It is interesting to learn how Leone approached the mood of the soundtrack for this particular film. Given much of it is to provide atmosphere to Noodles' thoughts and memories, the music is not overt, obvious or up-front. It is wistful, sad, melancholic, emotional in a different way, rather like the music one might hear in a dream. Leone himself said: "This time the emotions were so sharply defined, so strong and so romantic, that we agreed the music ought to be less emphatic than usual ... it ought to come from a long way away." This effect was certainly achieved. The music may have been played on speakers during filming, but we the viewer feel as if it's being played in Noodles' head, as he reflects on his life.

Morricone had been known to use the vocals of tenor Edda Dell'Orso in his musical soundtracks. But in Once Upon a Time in America, the human voice is more scarce than on his earlier and later scores. Morricone himself said: 'There is a reason why I used less of Edda dell'Orso's voice in this particular score, and it was right not to use it in the childhood scenes. The voice seemed perfect for moments which lament the passing of childhood, to lead the audience to think about times past – the thirty lost years of Noodles." When the voice is heard, it's mostly when Noodles is older, and it powers key emotional moments. In fact, it often makes them so moving they become overwhelming. Had the voice been more prominent all the way through, the impact would have dimmed.

Used sparingly however, it's heartbreakingly beautiful, the ghostly tenor singing from the past.

It's been reported that Ennio wrote all the music before the end of 1976, though it was recorded later of course. Yet up to the time of filming, Morricone would receive phone calls from a doubtful Sergio, who was in two minds about certain passages. Morricone recalled: "Sergio and I always think through our work to the very end, without ever declaring ourselves satisfied. Every so often, Sergio, when the music was already written, would phone me and say, Listen, let's have a quick meeting – because I'm beginning to have doubts about that theme for Deborah. Then he would listen to it, and calm down again. Because he still liked it, after all. This went on about every three months. And for the scriptwriters it seemed sometimes as if everything would become a crisis, and they would have to start doing everything all over again. With me, however, he just seemed to want his judgement confirmed every now and again.'

Much of the film was shot in Rome, at Cinecitta Studios, the hub of classic Italian film. There were shoots elsewhere too, like New York, Florida, Paris and St Petersburg. Somehow though, it all feels and looks like quintessential New York. It was in the Big Apple where Leone took the viewers back to the roaring twenties. In the Jewish neighbourhood of Williamsburg, Leone ensured not a trace of modern day life could be sniffed out.

In the end, after torturous casting sessions, Leone assembled an outstanding cast. Alongside De Niro as Noodles, it was James Woods who filled in the role of Max, Noodles' best friend. A dynamic and exciting actor, Woods would match De Niro's quiet intensity with a cobra like psychosis. He had already impressed audiences and critics in various films, especially 1979's seminal independent classic, The Onion Field, which features a frightening Woods performance. Here though, he was given one of the most important film roles of the period. Naturally, Woods gave it his all.

For James though, it had often been the case of not being the right guy for the part, and having to prove himself. Even in the 1990s, it has to be said, when he was well established, he still had to prove to directors like Oliver Stone and Rob Reiner that he had what it took. The fact he always convinced them he was good enough, committed enough, is a credit to him.

Speaking to Don Shewey in 1986, two years after the release of Once Upon a Time in America, and still hungry for more recognition, Woods explained how it had always been for him. "I worked my way up the ranks. I met a lot of resistance along the way; they always found a reason why they didn't want to use me. I wasn't conventionally good-looking or I was offbeat. The easiest thing in the world is for people out there to say no. To this day! They didn't want me for The Onion Field -- I wasn't right for the part. I had to pay for my own screen test. They didn't want me for Once Upon a Time in America -- I wasn't right for the part. Every movie I've ever gone up for, I wasn't right for the fuckin' part."

In the same interview, he spoke about the audition process for the film. "You would not believe the people who auditioned for Once Upon a Time in America. The biggest stars in the world fuckin' read for Sergio Leone. I said, Just let me do a screen test with De Niro. De Niro had thought I wasn't really right for the part, because the character was described as a blond Hercules. So I read this dialogue, and I said, I can do this better than anybody in the world. Bobby, because he's a great actor and knows what serves a movie well, said, Listen, I don't think he's right for the part, but let's give him a shot. We did this all-day screen test, and by the end of it they said, You're the guy. I can't tell you what a coup it was to get that part. Every actor in the world wanted to be in that movie. It was a very important step in my life."

William Forsythe would play Cockeye, one of the other four gangsters, while James Hayden took on Patsy. Joe Pesci, who had already become a firm De Niro friend after they starred in 1980s Raging Bull together, took on a small role as an Italian mobster name Frankie. According to some reports, Pesci wanted the Max role, but Leone was certain he wasn't right, and upon De Niro's advice cast him as Frankie instead. In the script, the Frankie role is much larger, though in the finished cut Pesci only has two scenes. Other notables in the cast included Rocky's Burt Young, a minor role as a gangster. Tuesday Weld was Carol, a bank teller who is raped by Noodles during a heist, and then becomes Max's lover and moll later on in the picture. Danny Aiello played a crooked police commissioner, while Treat Williams was cast as union leader Jimmy O'Donnell. On top of these, there were literally dozens of other roles, all played by actors who seem to have been born to play them.

Among the many character faces in the supporting cast is Robert Harper, who has a small role in the film as Sharkey. "I worked with the great Sergio Leone, who is more like a maestro with an orchestra," Harper told me in 2016, looking back on his experiences with Sergio. "We filmed in Italy with an Italian speaking crew and spoke an Italian version of English with Sergio. I was the new kid on the block; I had worked a couple of years earlier with Treat Williams on a Broadway revival of Once in a Lifetime, but I was also to be the "heavy" in a scene with experienced pros like Robert De Niro and James Woods. It would be accurate to say that I was nervous and not entirely confident on my first day. De Niro was already an enormous star, yet open and helpful; he made me feel comfortable. Sergio was very clear on what he wanted, always aware of the "big" picture. He has an acute eye and can watch numerous takes, noticing the smallest variations. He spoke to us as a group, as a conductor might guide the wind section, say. There was a formality and size..."

Actress Julie Cohen, who played the young Peggy in the childhood sequences, told me at length what it was like to work with Sergio.

"I was a young actress working in New York and got a call to audition for the film from my manager. I was 17 years old and had a background in theater and film acting," Cohen, now a musician, told me recently. "I liked the role when I read the audition sides; I thought the character of Peggy was sassy and funny. The role also made me nervous because of the sexual nature of the part and some nudity. But as an actor I'm drawn to taking risks. If a part scares me, it means I should take it. I was already beyond playing it safe, even at 17."

Her first memories of Sergio remain as vivid as the day she met him. "I remember my first meeting with Sergio Leone very clearly," she says. "It was my first audition for the film. I had the scenes in advance so I knew what I would be performing for the camera. What I didn't know is that he would answer the door in his bathrobe. The audition took place at a town house on the east side, near the UN. I think he was finishing breakfast and there was no rush. It was leisurely. He had large tortoiseshell glasses, a big belly, and a warm expressive manner. Although I was young and the material was somewhat racy, he made me feel at ease with his humour. He was watching everything I did very intently and commenting when I was too comic. He encouraged me to take the material seriously. I was cast in the role of young Peggy that day - one of the first people cast. But it would be another year before shooting began, which was lucky for me, I turned 18 in the meantime so I could travel to Italy on my own, without a guardian. My mother never forgave me.

"I had two different experiences of shooting Once Upon A Time in America," Julie continues. "In the US we filmed the exterior scenes; my scenes were shot in lower Manhattan, Chinatown and Soho. Coincidentally I lived nearby and could walk or take the subway to the set from home. One clear memory was the production department removing all television antennae from the rooftops to reflect the correct time period. Also, when we were shooting in the tenement building in Chinatown for the bathtub scene, it was very cold and I was nude, so the very considerate Italian crew would warm a robe for me with an iron so I could warm up between takes. Later I went to Rome to film interior scenes at Cinecitta, an incredible experience for any film fan. The history of that studio is remarkable and working there was an honour. One memory is the warm crusty focaccia bread brought to the set in the afternoon for a pick me up! Shooting in Rome was an amazing experience for an actor. The cast all stayed in the same hotel, sharing dinners and excursions. We became close, especially the kids in the cast.

"Sergio Leone was a great artist. This film was very important to him and he took it very seriously. He managed many aspects of the film - from tiny details to grand sweeping themes - shaping the material into a personal vision of American crime and punishment. Everyone working on the film was aware of his stature and gave him respect and trusted in his vision for the film. As an actor he made me feel safe and protected, a very fatherly figure. This is what a young actor needs, to feel safe enough to be vulnerable. Scott Tiler, Brian Bloom, Jennifer Connelly and I were all handing very adult material at a very young age, and it was Sergio's care and steady vision that made us feel safe enough to do that and make a better film full of heart and soul. I remember Sergio coaching Brian through the scene with the pastry beat by beat. The camera was running without sound and Sergio was sitting just out of the frame telling him when to move and how long to pause. It was as if he was painting or sculpting a human moment, using the actor as his clay."

People were used to their full potential on screen and picked with precision. De Niro actually helped out Leone in the casting department, and in the end there were 200 speaking parts. Behind the scenes, as good as the cast were, the film needed atmospheric flourishes to convincingly take you back to the age of the gangster and prohibition. Steven Kirshoff was on the set as special effects expert, there to add ambience and mood when needed. "I was hired to help with the effects in New York," Kirshoff, still in the industry, tells me today, thirty odd years down the line. "I did not have a ton of interaction with the director. Language was a bit of a problem. I mostly got instruction through the AD as I remember it. Steam and smoke, trash can fires are pretty basic. But he (Sergio) was interesting to watch at work, very intense as I remember it. Hard to compare him to anyone, but you could tell he was one of the great ones. He had that presence."

Amy Wells is now a set decorator for hit TV shows, but back in the early 80s, she wound up as assistant director on Leone's latest film by chance. "I came on for the New York shoot. I can't remember how I actually got the job on the film. I was hired as a set P.A., a job which I had never done. I was very, very green and knew almost nothing about being on a film set - the etiquette, how to use a walkie talkie, what the individual departments did. It was truly terrifying. The kicker was that many of the crew people were Italian and most of them did not speak any English. Several weeks into working Sergio decided that he was not going to join the Directors Guild of America (DGA), the reason being, as I understood it, was that it was $5000 and he didn't want to pay the money. All of the Assistant Directors that were DGA had to leave because it was no longer considered a DGA signatory and I was moved up with several other P.A.s to a higher position. I was made the NY second AD which was way way way over my experience level and would have been a difficult jump for any seasoned 2nd due to the period nature of the film, the amount of extras and the language gap."

No matter what you were doing on the set of Once Upon A Time in America, you were all kept in place, orchestrated if you like, by the master Leone. Sergio found the idea of finishing a film, as he so beautifully put it, "delicious"; but again in his own words, there is something slightly torturous about the making and editing of a movie, no matter how big or small it may be. In Leone's case however, it was as big as they came.

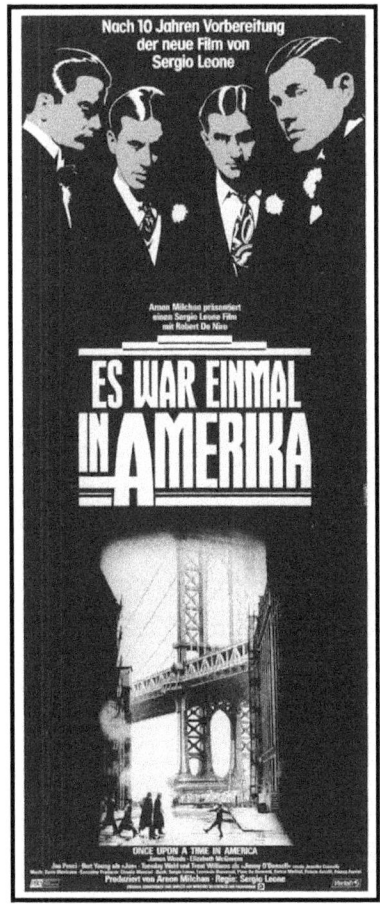

After filming was done, a famous Leone regular was recruited; the much loved poster artist Renato Casaro. Famed for his posters of Bond movies, Leone's spaghetti westerns and many more, he lent his trademark style to the art for Sergio's final film.

"Sergio Leone called me to create an international campaign for his movie, which was in post-production," Renato himself told me recently by email. "Leone and I had a long lasting relationship; he was trusting in me completely. I made several first scribbles on the concept, on which we discussed the way to go. After that I did a few sketches, of which two of them were chosen for the final artworks. I painted two versions, one very essential, the one with the golden faces, the other one in the way to tell the story of the movie. I wanted to transport the feeling that behind the beauty everything can happen; love and crime. The gangster-image arrives automatically if you have selected the right elements before. I think of Sergio very often. He was a man, and in his domain he was unique."

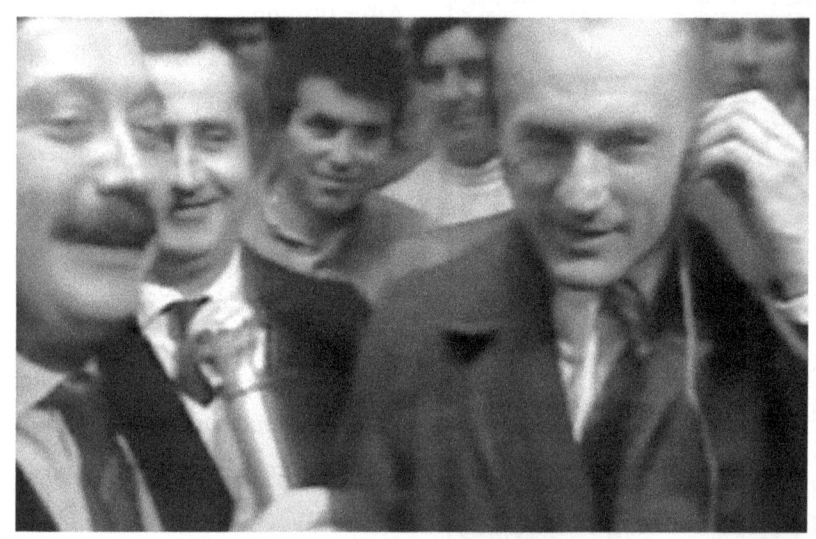

Above: De Niro, while made up as the aged Noodles, is interviewed for Italian TV on the film set. Below: Leone in the 1970s.

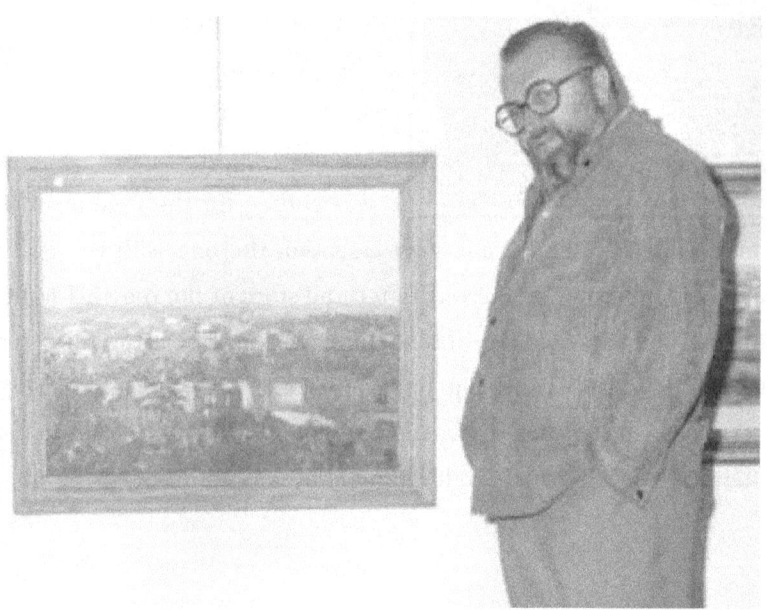

By the end of filming, Sergio realised he had ten hours of footage. It was all shot lovingly, every street corner view, every bit of strangely beautiful violence, every set piece, every dramatic scene. But as good as the footage was, there was simply no way he could have released a ten hour film, even if the devoted few would have devoured every single frame of it.

Sergio had a solution. He and his editor, Nino Baragli, would cut the film down to six hours, and release it in cinemas as two separate movies. But the studio was having none of this idea either. On a commercial level, this would have been suicide, and ruined the chances of such a glorious film getting the attention it truly deserved. On top of this, the studio only had to look back to an earlier Robert De Niro film to see how releasing a gigantic epic as two films meant box office poison. The film was 1900, directed by another Italian master, Bernardo Bertolucci (and scored, funnily enough, by Ennio Morricone himself). It had been put out in two halves, but according to some US reports few had bothered to turn up for part two. The Italy of 1900 is nightmarish, terrifying, ugly and bleak, a landscape of changing political values, the rise of fascism, where a dictator can freely go about his evil ways, killing cats, abusing and then murdering children at will. It is, in many ways, a fittingly repulsive film (though in my view something of a masterpiece), and anyone put off at the cinema by the first segment would surely have preferred to stay at home for the second. Bernardo saw it as a poem to Italy and it was an undoubtedly important work.

And though there are parallels between the two pictures (both are tales of friendship between two very different men), Once Upon a Time in America, though having its moments of true vile ugliness,

47

was on the whole a film of sincerity, melancholy and conscious style, every shot considered to the point that each one looked like a grand master's hand painted classic. This was a film made with love, and it showed in every single second. Still, releasing it in two parts might have limited its potential as a money maker in the eyes of the producers; and as much as he disliked the fact, commerciality had to be considered somewhere in the mix.

The first cut of the picture to please the studio came in at 4 and a half hours, but before it was due to be shown at the Cannes Film Festival, out of competition, Leone got it down to 3 hours and 40 minutes. You would think that would be the end of it (director finishes movie, gives it to the distributors and off it goes), but for Leone this was in some ways only the beginning, the start of many battles, each one more painful than the last.

His film, a piece of pure art, was handled like a piece of cheap product, sliced apart mercilessly by people who didn't understand his epic approach. James Woods told the New York Times that the film was "actually a movie. Not a merchandising opportunity. It was like doing Lawrence of Arabia. A huge movie. Impossible to explain how big it was." Yet here it was, being tossed around, being spoken of like a product, a commodity, a box of breakfast cereal.

For Leone it was heartbreaking. Though much of the rest of the world would embrace his fullest cut, the very country he was paying his most heartfelt tribute to, chewed it up and spat it out. It's been reported that during the first US screening of the full film, the projector broke ten minutes in, and more than a hundred people didn't even come back for part two.

"The Ladd Company panicked," Arnon Milchan said. "They changed the movie to a linear story, and cut an hour and a half. The movie that was released in the United States had nothing to do with the movie we made."

After such a long, stretched out period of pre-production and development, writing, casting, filming and arduous editing, there was a feeling of disenchantment, and Leone was drained by his experiences. But he made a truly great movie, one which would be more appreciated as time went on. Now, let's explore that movie…

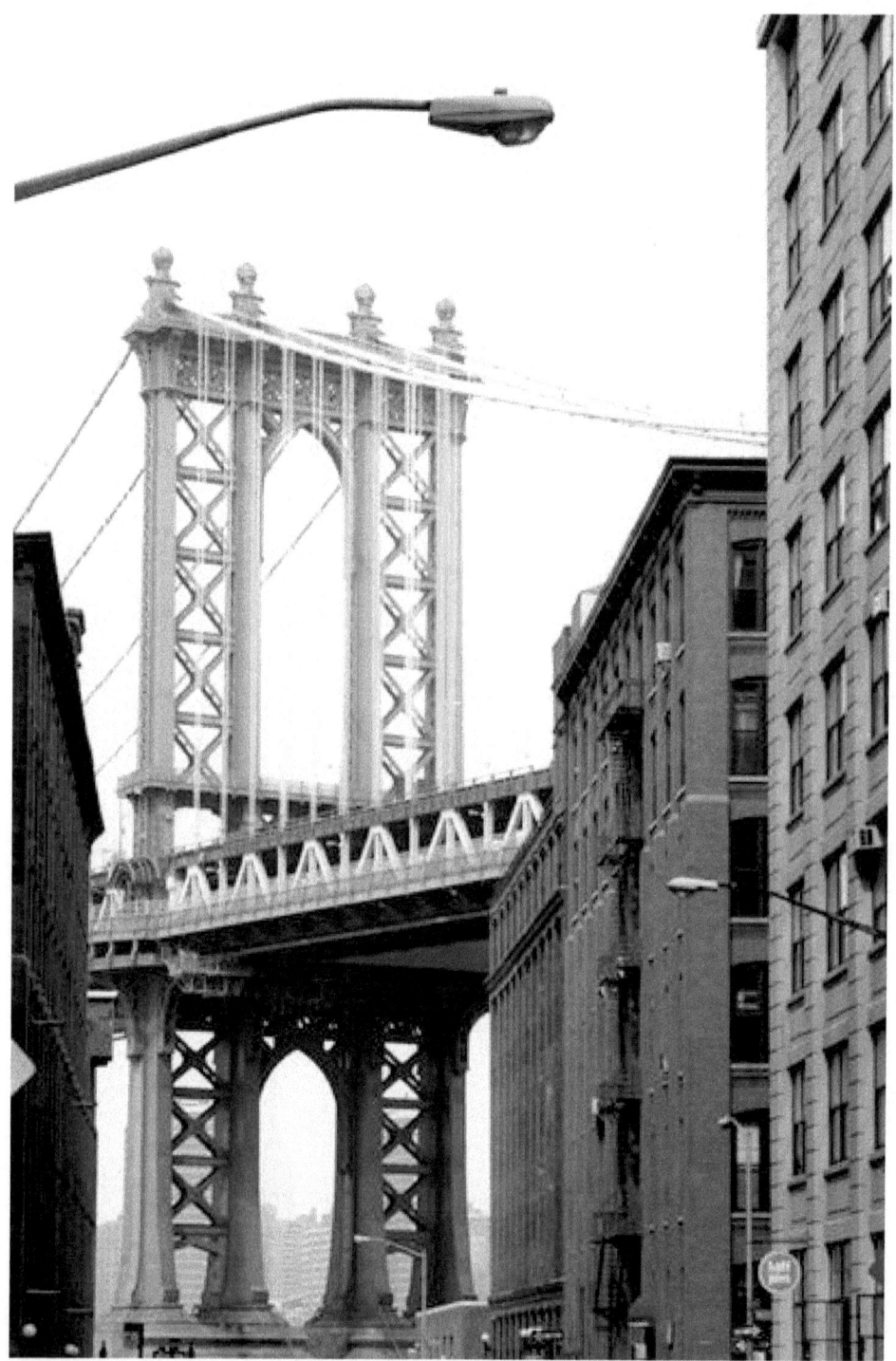

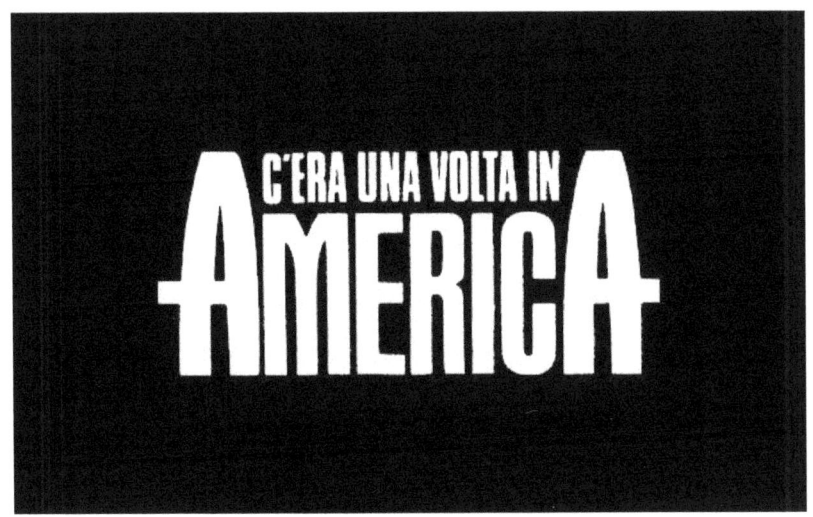

THEMES AND SUBTEXT

As a meditation on loss and regret, no motion picture can measure up to the towering stature of Once Upon a Time in America. A devastating, painful and at times extremely sad document of one man's attachment to his past, it's a film that - if we are talking about the full Leone cut of course - becomes soothing in a perverted fashion; the more melancholy and morose Noodles and his life becomes, the sweeter the film seems to be. No question, much of this mood was enhanced by the score of Morricone, who colours each sequence with the correct amount of sonic light, dark and shade. The shiver inducing pan pipe refrain returns again and again, but it's in the more beautiful passages, such as Deborah's Theme, where the music really takes us off to another place. To think that the producers forgot to enter Ennio's score into the Academy Awards is frustrating, angering even, for what is arguably the finest film score ever written and recorded would surely have bagged the Best Score gong.

But it's not just in the music where the film really grabs a hold of the heart. Despite the emotive, stirring, and often very sad score, somehow the movie never manipulates or leads the viewer towards a goal or an intended emotional destination. Instead, the actors and the director guide us in a direction where we can make our minds up about the characters and their fates, however deserved or not. The music, though extremely expressive and reflective of the scene in question, is simply another colour on the grand palette, another element of Leone's dream world.

To go through the plot can often feel like listing events upon events following one another rapidly, many in different time frames. On paper, the film looks like an unsolvable puzzle, and a synopsis would definitely put off potential viewers who like their films straight forward and without challenges. This said, when watching the events unfold before your eyes on the screen, the film does not seem like a disjointed, convoluted jumble of time jolts, flashbacks and possible dreams, but a cinematic experience like no other, pulling you into its strange, haunting atmosphere.

We start our journey of Noodles' life in the thirties, in an opium den in fact, where Noodles (De Niro) is flaked out. He envisions a flashback, a recent event in fact, of the police taking three bullet riddled bodies away from a crime scene in the pouring rain, as a phone rings and rings for what seems like an eternity on the soundtrack (all is revealed later of course). Meanwhile (the film's first sequence in fact), a group of gangsters go to his house and kill his moll. Searching for Noodles, they arrive at the opium den, but

Noodles is ushered out the back door and flees into the night. The young Fat Moe (Harry Knapp), friend to Noodles and his gang, is receiving a vicious beating by the gangsters, but he refuses to reveal Noodles' whereabouts. Later, while most of the gang go off in search of the "rat", Noodles arrives and blows one of the gangsters away, saving Moe's life. Noodles then retrieves a key from the grandfather clock in Moe's domicile and departs, leaving his bruised friend on the ground. When he learns that a large amount of money he expected to be located in a railway locker has gone, seemingly vanished, Noodles flees for Buffalo, buying a one way ticket with no plans to return.

We next find ourselves in 1968, when Noodles returns to Manhattan after years in hiding, old, droopy eyed and one-note. He returns to Fat Moe's restaurant with the news that someone has sent him a letter regarding arrangements for a "friend's" burial. Reuniting with Moe, we see how time has aged them. Later, Noodles gets the key to the railway locker (it is later revealed that Noodles and his gang set the locker up as kids to stash away their savings), opens it and finds a suitcase stuffed full of money. Apparently it's an advance on his next "job".

Between this, we are cast back to 1920, in Brooklyn, where Noodles and his gang are introduced as children. We meet the young Max, Cockeye and Patsy, plus other extended members of their circle, like Deborah, the object of Noodles' affection (played in the younger scenes by Jennifer Connelly, and by Elizabeth McGovern in the rest). Leone captures this era wonderfully. In with the beauty though are ugly truths. Theirs is a rough and ready world of crooked cops, rival gangs and sordidness. Getting their acts together, Max, Noodles and the boys quickly rise in the underworld, building up their reputations to take over their local area. Though there is affection between Noodles and Max, there is also a strange tension which often borders on hostility. Despite this, they are solid friends. But things then go awry, for Noodles that is. After stabbing a rival gang member to death for killing the youngest member of their group, Noodles is sent to prison.

He is released in 1932, now played by De Niro, where he meets back up with his old pals, while Max (James Woods) has clearly become the leader in getting the boys established as serious criminals, not just petty crooks. They run a bar in the prohibition era, bootlegging and being the "muscle" for union man Jimmy O' Donnell (Treat Williams).

In the adult scenes, there is even more of that tense rivalry between Noodles and Max, and though friendly, their respect for one another warps into competitiveness. Yet there is a strange brotherly love beneath the surface. The two differ drastically; Max wants the gang to be bigger, better and richer, while Noodles is happy for it to stay small time. He enjoys the life of crime; this is proven during a bank robbery where he viciously rapes a clerk, Carol (Tuesday Weld), who later becomes a high class hooker and then joins their extended gang, funnily enough as Max's lover.

As time goes on, Noodles' personality becomes more detached and wistful, and he starts to drift away from the others. There is one key event that changes it all. Still infatuated with Deborah, Noodles takes her out on a romantic date, hiring the whole restaurant for the night - an example of both his power and the fear he instils in people. They enjoy a perfect evening, but Deborah, now an aspiring actress, informs Noodles she is leaving for Hollywood the next day. Saddened, the date is over, and the pair end up in Noodles' chauffeur driven car. As the driver takes them homeward, Deborah tries to softly kiss Noodles, but he reacts by viciously raping her. In the near four hour cut, he actually rapes her twice, violently, with no regard for the pain he will be causing her. For him, this is a reckless act. She is leaving, and will be out of his life forever. He's asked her to stay and be his woman, but she knows life with him would be no fun, that he would lock her up and possess her as his toy. The rape then, is a destructive act, though in the long run the ordeal destroys him more than it does her. She experiences pain and horror at that moment, but his viciousness spurs her on in her career, and she later becomes successful, with Noodles just a face from the past. For him, the rape is a landmark moment, the point where it all goes wrong. It's a sickening display of carelessness which even Noodles himself appears to instantly regret upon finishing.

As she leaves to pursue her dreams the next day, Noodles watches her train depart the station. Haunted by his arrival, she glances at him blankly and simply pulls down the blind as the train chugs away, smoke permeating in the air. It's one of the most gut wrenching scenes in cinema history.

It is here when things really shift. Eventually Noodles returns to the gang. He has been away, drugging himself up in the opium den while Max and the gang are formulating their next plans, one of which is to rob the Reserve Bank, something which Noodles sees as certain suicide. Carol and Noodles plot to get the gang busted, seeing a small sentence for incited robbery preferable to death. Noodles rings the police and his friends, apparently, end up getting shot dead by the cops. He glumly watches as their bodies are taken away in bags. It is then we learn why Noodles left for Buffalo, not to return for thirty plus years.

In the latter day scenes, the haunted Noodles hears repeatedly of a Secretary Bailey, a name mentioned in a news report of the murder of the District Attorney. When Noodles visits the Bailey foundation, he is faced with an aged Carol, who tells him that the police tip-off that she and Noodles supposedly concocted was an idea instigated by Max all along. While there, Noodles spots a picture of Deborah on the wall, taken when the foundation first opened (Carol tells him she's a famous actress). He tracks her down and visits her in her dressing room, backstage, while she is appearing in a play. Done up in white face paint, which she gradually rubs off as the scene goes on, she appears to have not aged a day. This, of course, is how Noodles sees her, as the same beauty he let down all those years ago. She has aged of course, but we see her youthful looks through the eyes of a regretful old man still hopelessly in love.

When Noodles enquires about the identity of Bailey, Deborah is vague and becomes flustered when asked for information. He asks her whether he should take up the invite to visit the mysterious Secretary's house for a party. Deborah becomes increasingly edgy and nervous. Noodles now has an inkling that she and Bailey have lived together for years, but she cooks up a story of Bailey being an immigrant who got with a woman who died in childbirth. Becoming increasingly frantic, she advises Noodles not to go. As he leaves her dressing room, Noodles comes face to face with Bailey's son, who is the exact spitting image of a young Max (both parts are played by

Rusty Jacobs). It's another heart stopping moment in the film, handled beautifully by Leone in his slow zoom.

In the end, Noodles goes to the party, and though he never says it, he knows Bailey is the elderly Max. Max tells him the tale; that he faked his death and married Deborah, taking away from Noodles the one thing he always wanted. But Noodles doesn't rise to it. Given that he knows he is about to be assassinated, Max/Bailey urges Noodles to kill him. Asking his old friend to do the deed is his final offering to Noodles. But in Noodles' eyes, Max is already a dead man; after all, Max "died" all those years ago. He will not take up Bailey's offer and slowly leaves the mansion.

Noodles exits the mansion's grounds and heads up the dark, quiet street. Behind him, he hears a rubbish truck starting up. As it comes down the road towards him, Max (or someone resembling Max) appears from the gates of the mansion. Max marches towards Noodles, then the truck obscures him. When it drives onwards, Max is gone and nowhere to be seen. Noodles observes the truck as it passes him by, and it is clear that something freshly inserted in the mincer is now being crushed into tiny bits. Is it Max? Or has he faked his death once again? Deliciously, we never learn the truth. That's up to us.

The very last scene is a flashback to 1933, where Noodles is entering the opium den, removing his coat and getting comfortable as his drug is being neatly set up in a pipe for him. He begins to puff away, and float off to his happy place. The film ends with a close up of Noodles' grinning face, a strange, contorted grin that shows us the tortured man at his most content. The credits roll over his goonish smile, eyes crinkled in glee.

Though long, Once Upon a Time in America simply flies by, and one cannot help but feel like putting it on again as soon as it's over. There is a totality to it, an eternal feeling. Yet it also feels like a puzzle that finally seems to be solving itself at the very end, only for a new, even more befuddling and teasing mystery to hit you face on.

Though there is so much I admire and ponder upon about this film, one thing that really lasts in the memory is Max's perverse manipulation of Noodles. To the very end, Max seemingly wants to confuse, bewilder and torture Noodles, getting one over on him at every opportunity; until of course he wants to give him the gift of killing him. But Noodles is a man living in the past, refusing to admit he has been fooled for the past thirty odd years. It's so much easier to deny Max is still among the living and masquerading himself as Bailey, for his very existence underlines how wasted and pointless Noodles' life has been.

And just what the hell has Noodles been up to all this time? He tells Moe he's been "going to bed early", so we imagine a man living a paranoid, twitchy, reclusive existence all alone. For all those years, was Noodles a tortured, embittered, desperately sad man, constantly peering over his shoulder for the click of a gun in his ear?

"You're still acting like a street schmuck! You know, if we'd listened to you, we'd still be rolling out drunks for a living!"

Once Upon a Time in America is among the richest and most dense films of all time, and to discuss every scene and theme in detail would take a ten volume series. But in the following sections I will explore certain areas of the film which I feel offer the viewer a window into understanding the picture's more mysterious, ambiguous qualities.

We can start with its main star. At the centre of this film, as our guide through the underbelly of 20th Century America, is Robert De Niro. Noodles is possibly the most complex character De Niro has ever played, and you only have to glance through his filmography and remember those characterisations, those intense performances, to see that Noodles is a total mystery in the midst of them all. Placing Noodles within his oeuvre is rather useful in highlighting this fact.

One of his most famous performances, perhaps his most celebrated, is as Jake La Motta in Martin Scorsese's Raging Bull, the pinnacle of acting to which all else is judged against. One can "understand" the sheer monstrous savagery of Jake La Motta, but still not condone a single aspect of it. De Niro won an Oscar for his turn as the controversial boxer, and it was a fearless, no punches pulled (no pun intended) portrayal of a nightmarish bully, a violent man who can't find peace in any area of his life. There were no complications here, no underlying motives. La Motta is nasty, plain and simple, a destructive primal being intent on pushing away everyone who is capable of loving him. Though we don't like him, he is what he is, and there are no airs and graces. Nothing is hidden, all is exposed; his rage, his violence, his pettiness, his paranoia, his jealousy, his egotistical tendencies. La Motta is what it says on the tin, unlike Noodles.

Looking at other unhinged De Niro performances and you will see many are as clear as day. Max Cady, the demented rapist and killer De Niro would play in Martin Scorsese's 1991 thriller Cape Fear, is one of De Niro's broadest psychos, a Southern horror monster; creepy, darkly charming (when he wants to be) and terrifying in equal measures. It was a blistering performance, but again, Cady was clearly the villain of the piece, and we had no sympathy for him whatsoever. In this case, the guy who looked like the bad guy *was* the bad guy.

All De Niro performances, especially the heavier ones, have an underlying river of intensity beneath them. It's those piercing eyes that show us there is often a lot more going on under the surface than above it. He may be doing very little externally, but the darkness, the sadness, the rage, or whatever the character is harbouring, is there behind the mask. Even in his most enigmatic performances however, you can still read him. Taxi Driver's Travis Bickle is clearly an isolated odd ball, a man who wants human connection but pushes it away every time it comes near. Like La Motta, he too is a self destructive being; only Bickle is introverted, for the most part punishing only himself, until his violent explosion at the end. Whereas La Motta was a man driven by his own selfishness, mentally and physically abusing all around him, Bickle mentally tortures the man in the mirror. He becomes an angel of death, saving the teenage prostitute Iris (Jodie Foster) as an act of redemption, killing the vile pimp, Sport (Harvey Keitel), and releasing her, and himself, from the urban horrors of New York City. It's the psychopath's second coming.

When we come round to his turn as Noodles, perhaps his most underrated performance in my view, we realise what a complex, detailed and concise piece of work it really is. As the Sabotage Times quite rightly put it, "In The Godfather, Marlon Brando played Don Corleone as a charismatic pantomime villain. In America, Robert De

Niro's Noodles is a man with so many contradictions and insecurities, he makes Travis Bickle seem as simple as Forrest Gump."

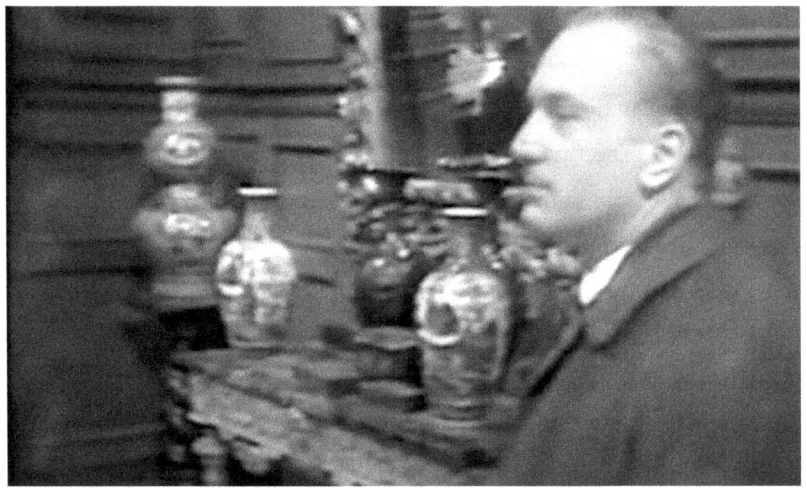

De Niro as the ageing Noodles, just before a take on set

Noodles is a deep man, as deep as a black ocean, and one can see intense thought, sadness and contemplation in his eyes throughout. As a young mobster, he often seems to be "one of the boys", enjoying himself in the gang's frolics. Whether it be womanising, robbing or drinking, for a while Noodles is happy to be a part of it. Then, troubled by the unrequited love for Deborah, something breaks off, and he desires to be alone. He'll take his coat, his face will drop and he will appear glum. The man needs his solitude, even in his younger years as a high flying gangster. He yearns for his own time, but seems to resent such moments and needs too. Like Bickle, the man who alienates himself and then complains of feeling alienated, Noodles is the self punishing male, existing on the fringes out of choice and then appearing regretful of the fact. He rapes Deborah and wonders why they never ended up together.

As an older man, long coat and hat covering his tired face, Noodles is a ghost of a long gone era. He roams the streets, slowly, calmly, passing construction workers, rowdy youths playing basket ball and graffiti like it's the first time he's laid his eyes on such things. To him, the New York he knew is long gone and all that remains is a shattered, fractured shell. The glory years are behind him.

We do not pity him, even if we do care, for Noodles is too deeply flawed to be relatable. De Niro makes him multi faceted though, and nothing here is black and white. There are a few scenes which really capture how emotionally stunted and self centred Noodles really is. When he first emerges in 1968 New York and enters Fat Moe's bar, we see the sheer glee and joy on Moe's face. "Noodles!" he exclaims, so happy to see his friend after thirty five years. In response, Noodles is distant, if not blank, externalising no emotion or acknowledgment whatsoever. "Lock the door," he says, making it clear that the years in hiding have made him cautious and cold.

> *"I'm not that kind of guy. Besides, I'm afraid if I give you a good crack in the mouth, you'd probably like it..."*

There's a repeated pattern in the classic filmography of Robert De Niro, and that is that his characters are often clueless and totally estranged from the mysteries of the female. They also tend to have a very warped idea of love and relationships, which adds depth to the portrayals. As Noodles, De Niro is enraptured by Deborah, but he doesn't know how to treat her on a man to woman level. Hiring out restaurants and romanticising her is all well and good, but it is not the basis of a proper relationship, nor is it a way to form a real bond. When they lie together after their grand meal on the grass, it's one of the most beautiful, simple and watchable scenes in the whole film. One can gaze at the shots forever, but this is merely a calm before the storm. The sickening rape scene, for me the turning point of the picture, is harrowing, extremely disturbing, seemingly never ending and, it has to be said - especially the first time you see it - very upsetting. Only moments before he begins his violent attack in the back of the car, as the streets go by behind them, Deborah is seen leaning forward towards him and giving him a warm kiss. He does not respond to it, his eyes are filled with disdain and anger, for he knows what he is about to do.

After he rapes her once, he immediately starts again. The camera angles do not spare us the horror of this vile sexual degradation. Close ups show vicious thrusts that are done through anger and resentment, yet while he achieves his climax, he grabs and holds her like it were the most beautiful moment of his life. There's a strangeness to his embrace, of brief ownership, as if Noodles knows that after this he won't see her again and he had better make the sick, twisted moment last. Clutching her romantically as he thrusts his final thrusts, the viewer is left nauseated by his act. Deborah lies there in a heap, her pretty dress torn, her face red and puffed up with the tears. Noodles gets out into the early morning air, hands on hips, and seems ashamed of himself. When the driver comes over (played by the film's producer, Arnon Milchan), Noodles attempts to give him some money. "Take her home," he says, holding out a wad of money. The driver shakes his head in disgust and rushes back to the car. Not everyone can be bought with money, it seems.

As if we didn't already know it by previous scenes involving Noodles and women, it is clear that the man is incapable of treating women right. He is also incapable, it seems, of engaging in conventional sex. If we go back to the childhood sequences, he is almost fiendish in his girl-ogling ways, a lecherous reptile looking through holes. When he attempts to have sex with the Young Peggy, he is forceful and aggressive. Even in his youth, it seems, Noodles was a man for whom consented sexual pleasure was off the cards. And it's also clear that his sexual desire goes hand in hand with his violent tendencies, with both urges often overlapping as part of one experience. (We need only think of him having sex with the woman in the hearse to grasp the symbolism in Leone's sex/death metaphor.)

The other big rape scene, though not as disturbing as the one inflicted on poor Deborah, is the one involving De Niro and Tuesday Weld as Carol in the bank. Carol begs Noodles to hit her, so he does, but then he hits her with something more brutal. Bending her over a desk, he rapes her from the back. At first she screams, calls him names and struggles to get away; but after a while, she clearly starts to enjoy it. It shifts the scene into the controversial yes/no territory (think of Peckinpah's Straw Dogs). When she later turns up again as a high class hooker, and meets the gang in a back room, she is a changed woman, freed from her sexual shackles. In an attempt to identify the one "she got to know better" earlier in the film, in the back room she uses up-close and personal methods to identify the guilty man. She guesses wrong, and is drawn immediately to Max. De Niro then watches as Weld and Woods start to kiss passionately. She even invites De Niro along for the ride. He turns her down, disgusted by the idea of a threesome, and leaves the room. This highlights Noodles' double standards; saying "I'm not that kind of guy" to a group sex session, but happily raping his true love, highlights the contradictory traits of this very strange man.

If Noodles uses women as toys or playthings, he does so because it's there in the script. Indeed, it has to be said that Leone's treating and handling of women in the film in general, whether they are molls, hookers or everyday women, is shabby to say the least. Of course, this was deliberate, and Leone was merely presenting women as they had always been shown in the gangster genre. Who can forget the classic scene in The Public Enemy for instance, when James Cagney roughs up his missus by shoving a grapefruit in her face? Still, that's light in comparison to the way "broads" get it in Once Upon A Time in America. If you look through the film, no women are treated with respect. Of course, this was the way it was in the gangster world, and one has to accept this when going in to view the picture. This was no place for radical feminism. It seems pointless then, to call out the role of women within the context of the film as problematic. After all, how can you show violent men without the violence?

When asked by American Film, rather ridiculously, if he had anything against women, Leone was sharp and straight to the point. "I have nothing against women, and, as a matter of fact, my best friends are women," he said, outraged. "What could you be thinking? I tolerate minorities. I respect and kiss the hand of the majorities, so you can just about imagine then how I genuflect three or four times before the image of the other half of the heavens. I even, imagine this, married a woman, and, besides having a wretch of a son, I also have two women as daughters. So if women have been neglected in my films, at least up until now, it's not because I'm misogynist, or chauvinist. That's not it. The fact is, I've always made epic films and the epic, by definition, is a masculine universe."

In 1987, Leone made even more interesting points about the role of women in his movies. Though they exist outside the very male world which dominates the flow of the film, this fact in some ways makes them more powerful, more liberated, and less chained to the life of crime which the men are destined for.

"Would you like to know why I create the women as I do?" Leone said. "Well, because I think women have always been considered objects, especially in the genre of westerns. And especially in gangster films, with the gangster's moll—she would always be more or less of an object. And I'm not convinced of this theory. Because I think even gangsters' women have brains. They think and even, as we say, have balls. When I used Claudia (Cardinale) for example, in Once Upon a Time in the West, she represented the birth of American matriarchy. Because women had enormous weight in America. And they still have. Because they are truly the padrone (owners, masters) of America. Therefore, when they are put into a film, I think they have to be put in for a distinct purpose and have a reason to exist. Not as some superficial or gratuitous presence. You see in Once Upon a Time in the West the whole film moves around her (Cardinale). If you take her out, there's no more film. She's the central motor of the entire happening. It's the same for Deborah and for Carol in Once Upon a Time in America."

A look through the female characters though, once you get over the alleged sexism, shows interesting, varied and imaginative attention to detail. Carol may be raped by Noodles during the robbery, but it seems that the rape itself ignited something within her she may have not known about before. When she asks Noodles to hit her, she is inviting his brutality, and in this way of thinking, she is no longer overpowered or dominated. In a strange way, she has slapped him and forced him into degrading her, as she obviously wishes him to. She treats him as much like an animal as he does her. When the gang meet with her later in the back room of the bordello, she is a sexually powered being who chooses Max out of the line up of men. She then leaves her husband, and hooks up with Max full time. Typically, Max treats her like trash, as evident in one particular scene (His comments, "I don't give a shit about her" and "SHUT UP!" say it all) when Max tries to convince Noodles that women still don't matter much in their world. Yet in her next scene, there she is, right beside Max.

But Deborah is the most important female character in the film, as Leone said the central motor. Head over heels in love with her since childhood, there is a painful longing in the eyes whenever De Niro's Noodles is in her company. As children, he worships her, but sees her as unobtainable. In the 30s sequences, she is almost in reach, but she chooses the promise of stardom over life as a gangster's moll; very wisely it must be added, especially when you consider what happens to Noodles' girlfriend at the beginning of the movie. Deborah is the one woman who stands her ground, says she wants more out of this life and follows her dreams. (Perversely of course, in the end she becomes Max's woman, an ironic twist if there ever was one.) The hideous rape scene finishes off Noodles' chances, and had he had any sense at all, he would have quit the crime life, straightened up and gone to Hollywood with her. The saddest part is that Deborah clearly loves Noodles, deep down, and you can see it in her eyes. But what comes back from Noodles is more muddled. Yes he loves her too, but he knows they don't fit together. She is the ambitious beauty, so pure and "perfect" to him, while he is the rough and ready crook, capable of so much badness that he knows in his heart he doesn't even deserve such a woman. Is the rape a deliberate, self destructive act, a way for Noodles to ensure he never attempts to change and step up to the plate? Like his Travis Bickle in Taxi Driver, he demolishes any hope that ever comes into his life by making his angel into a whore (ala Betsy in Taxi Driver, and the trip to the porno theatre), spoiling her purity. He is that breed of alienated male who side lines himself recklessly, preferring the solitude of melancholy loneliness over blissful peace, to wallow in his own self pity.

When he does meet up with Deborah again in the late sixties, she is just as fresh faced, beautiful and perfect to him as she was in the 1930s. As she rubs off the stage make up, her face remains the same. To him, it's 1933 again, and Deborah is that sweet young woman on her way to Hollywood and out of his life. What Deborah now feels for Noodles though is anyone's guess. Nothing is really said of the matter, but one can see the sadness in her eyes too. It's a beautiful scene, De Niro the crumbling, aging old man, and Deborah the unchanged, youthful flower.

McGovern herself felt that certain things got in the way of her fully enjoying the experience of making the film. She felt the childhood sequences were perfect, but that the adult scenes never really measured up. "There was this feeling that Sergio and De Niro were on slightly different tracks," she admitted. "De Niro was so interested in realistic detail and was often concerned that there wasn't enough of it, and Sergio could not have been less interested... They were both after creating a good piece of work, so I suppose it was the best kind of fight. I did feel pulled between them, De Niro was such a strong presence and Sergio's English was not so good. Sometimes I think I lost track of who I was and what I wanted to do. It's such a male film and Deborah, on top of that, is blatantly a man's vision of a woman, a very hard thing to know how to fulfil if you're not the one having the vision, if you're the object."

The most famous scene in McGovern's career has to be that rape scene. Looking back, she said it was actually the easiest scene to film, somewhat ironically. But she also felt the scene had ramifications. While sexism is often brought up by critics looking at the movie's flaws, it is interesting to note McGovern's views on the film and her role in it.

"In terms of acting, that scene was, in some ways the easiest of all," McGovern told the Independent. "There was something very clear to react to. It was incredibly easy to understand, incredibly easy to do. My feeling about that scene, and I hate to admit it, was just 'Oh thank God, I don't have to do any acting, at least I know what I'm doing here. At least I don't feel confused about what I'm supposed to play.' In some ways I feel as though the entire experience of making the film, or maybe that entire period of my life was represented in that scene. I was this young person, incredibly like Deborah. I had a lot of ambition and drive and I was in a position where I was viewed by the world in a way that had nothing to do with reality, much the same way as Noodles has this image of Deborah. You're being used and you feel used. I suppose many young girls would think of it as the most wonderful thing in the world, to be this hot young movie star that people have sexual or romantic fantasies about, but in fact you learn very quickly that who you are is nothing to do with what their projection of you is. I look back on that whole period of being an object, being someone else's fantasy, as not very nice. I'm relieved not to be that any more. I look back on that period of my life, and the rape was sort of a metaphor for what it felt like."

Carol and Deborah are not the only female characters worth discussing. Peggy, though a minor character, is an important one too. As a child, she is happy to indulge the boy's sexual fantasies in exchange for a cream cake. As a woman grown up, she has gotten chubbier, and is now a madam, selling her own and other's flesh for money. In the scene where Noodles comes out of prison and into the bar, she is delighted to see him. He is pleased too, and proceeds to "enjoy" her breasts. The mood is jovial and light, coarse even, but when the four gangsters leave the bar for the back room, Peggy (played by Amy Rider as an adult) looks sad. She sighs and leans on the side. Is it possible she too harbours feelings for Noodles? Or is there more to it than that? Is she slightly regretful that no one really views her as a "woman" in her own right, but a piece of loose flesh there to grab and grope when anyone pleases? It's a vital moment I feel, but one so brief that it at first appears to be irrelevant. Her expression symbolises the doom of the moll, the floozy, the woman in the midst of the gangster's life.

When Noodles accepts Deborah is gone forever, he hooks up with a young woman, though he appears to have considerably less interest in her. He actually treats her well to be honest, but his heart does not pulsate for her as it did for Deborah. Eve (Darlanne Fluegel) gets "whacked" early on, but she is seen later in flashback. During a holiday, Eve comforts Noodles on the beach as Max goes off on a psychopathic rant, and later appears to be heartbroken when Noodles announces he is leaving. In many ways, she is the most conventional female part in the film, and definitely the most stable. Though her role is small, it's a good addition, and indeed a nice twist on the life and inevitable fate of the gangster's moll.

For a director who confessed to be concerned with the world seen through the eyes of the male, he certainly gave us mixed and illuminating examples of womanhood to consider; the moll, the nympho, the madam and the morally decent. Sure, they were male ideas of femininity, but as these women were surviving in a cruel, macho, unforgiving world, it is important we view them from a distance, through the insensitive eye of the mobster. But the term "fairer sex" never sounded so incorrect.

"Don't you ever call me crazy!"

James Woods is tremendously good as Max. To say he is a screen psychopath though, may be simply cataloguing him as another mad man. Like Noodles, Max is a complex, multi faceted person, a figure of contradictions. He is ambitious, cold, heartless, but very clever. There is admiration for Noodles too, and this is clear whenever Max looks at him. There is a love there, but it's battling against something else; an ego driven jealousy, always feeling the need to compete with his contemporary. After all, throughout the film he ends up getting whatever or whoever Noodles wanted.

In the childhood scenes, Noodles is promised sex from Peggy, but he proves inept and Max takes it instead. Later, Noodles rapes Carol, but Carol ends up coupled up with Max. Most importantly of all though, is the way Max takes Deborah from him. They have had a life together, while Noodles has been in the dark, hiding himself away from the world. It is Max's main pursuit and aim in life to do one over on Noodles, to better him and surpass him in everyway. There is also an ironic twist. While Noodles has been in hiding to conceal his identity, Max changes his own identity by choice - and whole life in fact - to achieve power in an all new way. He knows that politics is not so dissimilar from the world of organised crime, and the fact they so obviously overlap. Max uses his wits and knowledge of the streets to enforce his way to the top in another jungle. In truth, it was probably the most natural, seamless transition for him. But by the film's end he is a man who has run out of options, run out of time, and who knows the game is up. While he must face the music and the inevitability of his own death, Noodles can walk away with his anonymity intact.

Woods had given good performances before he took on Once Upon A Time in America, but he hadn't broken through yet. He had a lot of experience on the stage, and had been making films since 1972. Woods rose to prominence with his powerful and acclaimed performance as the cop killer in The Onion Field (1979), an early sign that he was a daring, bold and exciting performer, unpredictable and dynamic. By the time he had filmed his role as Max in Leone's epic, he took on the starring part in David Cronenberg's mind bending Videodrome (1983) and went on to become one of Hollywood's most versatile, arresting and reliable character actors.

He was Oscar nominated and absolutely brilliant in Oliver Stone's Salvador (1986), as a sleazy photojournalist in too deep, a man searching tirelessly to capture the truth on film, despite the fact he was unable to tell the truth in his personal life. He has given many stunning performances down the years; just think of his award winning turn in 1986's TV movie Promise, a moving portrayal of a man wanting a normal life but too mentally ill to live one; his lead roles in Cop, The Boost, Best Seller and John Carpenter's Vampires; in a totally improvised role in Martin Scorsese's Casino; as the mild father in The Virgin Suicides; or his film stealing turns in Any Given Sunday, The Specialist and The Getaway. He is always a compulsively watchable force (during our interview I mentioned the word feral when we talked about his acting, and Woods liked my description), but for me his tour de force as Max is one of the greatest performances of 1980s cinema.

"I was a still-to-be-proven character actor on the cusp of some kind of success," Woods said in a recent interview, "playing opposite the most widely acclaimed actor in the world. I just thought that my challenge was to go toe-to-toe with him in every scene and prove I'm of the same mettle as him. I pursued the challenge of being in an ego competition to infuse the relationship between Max and Noodles with the same sense of affection and yet dire competition. And Bobby was aware of it, and it was good for the film."

But Woods learned a lot from working on the film, especially from Leone, who he considers one of the greats in the history of filmmaking. "The greatest compliment I ever got was from Sergio Leone," Woods told Den of Geek. "He said 'I've always worked like an opera director. My actors are props'. Wonderful actors! Henry Fonda,

Jason Robards people like that! But he said they're like props. He said 'I have the entire scene worked out, tell them where to stand, the camera moves, I have an image of how they're going to be, and they're living storyboards.' But he called us 'wild boys', and I asked him why. He said 'You guys come in, I say do this, you say no, I want to do this, and I'm now in a position of covering what you do, but it's more fun than I've ever had'.' He said, 'I can plan one thing, but then you do something and I come up with shots that I like even better, because the action makes more sense sometimes than what I'd planned'. It was a great compliment to have Sergio Leone say, You make me a better director."

Woods has played quite a few psychotic and narcissistic characters in his career following Leone's film. One of my personal favourites of his turns is in Killer: A Journal of Murder (1995), in which he plays real life serial killer, Carl Panzram. Carl is a nasty bastard through and through, and Woods goes in fearlessly. During the flashback scenes which depict him killing, he is more monster than man, at one point turning to camera, almost growling and foaming at the mouth. But in his strange and unlikely friendship with a kindly guard, Woods reveals the concealed humanity of a man who was never loved. As James once said himself (on Inside the Actor's Studio to be precise), even killers get haemorrhoids, and Woods is an expert at turning characters that others might have made one dimensional into believable, multi faceted men.

As for revealing the humanity in his most vile characters, his Byron De La Beckwith, an Oscar nominated turn in Ghosts of Mississippi, might be an exception; the man is pure evil from top to bottom. But

Woods does not do caricature. Even when he is the Hollywood villain, his performances are not without appeal and humour.

The mad eyed, conniving, often explosive Max is the polar opposite to Noodles' slow, mannered and downplayed manner. Woods knew he had to match De Niro, and seeing as De Niro was playing it subtle and understated, Woods was aware the best thing to do was match that calm with intensity. That said, he never goes overboard, and stays within a parameter, but he certainly lends Max a terrifying charm. When he does blow up, he is frightening, lashing out at Noodles like a wild beast. He keeps his anger deep inside, but when it boils over, you can be sure everyone knows about it. Just don't call him crazy!

"I like the Stink of the Streets..."

There have been gangster movies since almost the very start of cinema itself; even the pioneer DW Griffiths himself made mob films, such as The Musketeers of Pig Alley. But it wasn't really until the talkie era that it fully expanded into a serious crowd drawing genre. For me, and many others of course, James Cagney was the king of the gangsters, and the run of mobster flicks he made are unmatched today; The Public Enemy (1931), Angels With Dirty Faces (1938), The Roaring Twenties (1939), White Heat (1948) and lots more in between define an age. Of course, Edward G Robinson and others helped boost the gangster's popularity, but it was Cagney who stands the test of time. This was the age of the star, the contracted movie idol, and though there were some well celebrated directors, filmgoers flocked to see their heroes (or anti-heroes) on the big screen, not the guy controlling the cameras.

After the golden age, the mob film kind of slipped out of view. Sure, there were gangster films still being made, but few had the true class of the classics. The Brotherhood, released in 1968 and starring Kirk Douglas, was one of the highest profile gangster films of the 1960s, but it was a massive flop for Paramount. When the rights to the hit book The Godfather by Mario Puzo were bought, few predicted box office success for what they saw as a slightly schlocky gangster story. With young buck Francis Ford Coppola as director, and unwanted stars in the likes of Al Pacino and Marlon Brando (Coppola had to fight to get Paramount to accept his lead actors, and risked his job on a daily basis), The Godfather was seen as an inconsequential little movie. Budgeted at 7 million, it became one of the biggest hits of its time, raking in 250 million at the box office, a staggering amount even in today's money.

All of a sudden, there were hundreds of gangster scripts flying all over the place. In the wake of The Godfather's massive success, many of these scripts were brought to the screen. Even if some of them were hits, few have lasted and stood the test of time. Pictures like Capone (1974) represented the watchable, low budget exploitation side of the gangster revival, with producer/director Roger Corman jumping quickly on the bandwagon. (You also have to note two key early 70s Corman crime films; Bloody Mama (1970), featuring a young De Niro; and Boxcar Bertha (1972), directed by a pre-Mean Streets Martin Scorsese.) The studios made many a gangster picture too, like The Don is Dead (1973) and The Outfit (1973), but it was to be an independent film which turned the camera away from the high class dignitary of the likes of the Corleones and on to the petty, rough and ready, lower class charm of the street hoods.

Martin Scorsese, who had made his personal film Who's That Knocking At My Door (1967) and the picture for Corman, Boxcar Bertha (1972), finally put together his dream project in 1973, the startling and highly influential Mean Streets. Starring Harvey Keitel as a small time gangster on the cusp of greatness, Charlie finds himself torn between his Catholic guilt, his foolhardy friend Johnny Boy (Robert De Niro in his breakthrough performance) and the fact he is about to be welcomed into the mob hierarchy any time soon if he plays his cards right. Mean Streets took viewers down into the streets of Little Italy, through the bars, on to the sidewalks and into the life of a small time crook.

Though it wasn't an instant hit, it got rave notices and as the years went by, and De Niro and Scorsese's fame ballooned, the film grew in popularity. Mean Streets is a watershed moment for the gangster genre. It took us back to the grittiness of the classic gangster films of the 1930s, but it pulled no punches and refused to paint a glamorous portrait of the duality of violence and glory. As wonderful as The Godfather was, the scenes of violence were stylised in a way to make them cinematic. Coppola, a famous hater of movie violence, made sure that if there had to be violence in his movies, or grizzly killing for that matter, then each scene would be properly thought out. It wasn't just killing for killing's sake; Coppola had to stage each bloody sequence and make it unique. Mean Streets, in contrast, took us into the middle of bar room fist fights, with shaky camera work and rowdy crowds. It was far from perfection, more like a street documentary than a stylised cinematic feast for the eyes. When De

Niro's Johnny Boy is shot at the end of the film, it's one of the most hideous and startling shoot out scenes in the history of cinema.

Though there were numerous mob films throughout the rest of the 1970s, apart from the Godfather sequel, very few stand out as prime examples of the genre. In my view, it isn't until Once Upon a Time in America that we truly get to see a new slant on the mobster film. While The Godfather was epic, it was also a group piece. Though Brando was the true star, he wasn't really on screen that much, and as the film moves towards the end, Pacino becomes the central figure in the plot. Also in the mix are James Caan, Robert Duvall, John Cazayle, Diane Keaton, Talia Shire and many others, all of whom contribute fine performances of varying size and depth. In comparison, Once Upon A Time in America is really a film about one man, alone on a hopeless quest for himself through life. There are numerous characters who come in who are greatly important to the story (most of all Max of course, as well as Deborah), but Noodles is who we go along with on this fifty year trek through time. And he is certainly no Don Corleone.

For a man who has played very few gangsters, it's funny to think that Robert De Niro is seen as the ultimate screen gangster. If you look at his vast (and steadily growing) filmography, the mobster roles are actually few and far between. In the 1970s, he played a gangster disguising as a priest in The Gang That Couldn't Shoot Straight (1971), Johnny Boy in Mean Streets, and the young Vito Corleone in Coppola's Oscar winning follow up, The Godfather Part 2 (1974). In the latter, Pacino plays Michael Corleone in the 1950s, becoming more corrupt and twisted as his empire grows, which works in stark contrast against the flashback scenes, starting at the turn of the century, when the young Vito comes to America from Sicily. De Niro's scenes are romantically lit, almost dream like, and his Vito is a man of honour, courage and respect, who works his way up through snubbing out the local bully gangster who extorts the workers. It's a wonderfully mannered and controlled performance by De Niro, spoken entirely in Sicilian, and is one of his warmest roles to date.

In the 1980s, apart from his role as Noodles, he played Al Capone in The Untouchables (1987), and a criminal, again, disguised as a priest in the underrated comedy, We're No Angels (1989). It was in the 1990s that De Niro played his highest profile mobsters for years, in Scorsese's dual masterpiece whammy of Goodfellas (1990) and Casino (1995). Again, they were gangsters, but they were fully rounded characters too, and greatly different from one another. His Jimmy Conwy in Goodfellas is a twitchy, seedy crook, a mentor to the younger Henry Hill (Ray Liotta), who can never be a "made man" due to his Irish blood. De Niro embodies the shifty, aging criminal with ease. His Sam "Ace" Rosthein in Casino is a celebrated bookie for the mob who gets appointed as the head of their new Vegas casino. Though happily letting his wild friend Nicky (Joe Pesci) enforce violence on those who cross him, Sam wants to be a straight business man. He never performs an act of violence himself throughout the movie, and though he is at times very questionable, he still comes out as possibly the most decent and incorrupt guy in the whole movie - which says something about the other guys in the film for sure.

Since then, De Niro has often spoofed his gangster image, and played the criminal for laughs in films like Analyze This (1999),

Analyze That (2002), A Shark Tale (2004), and The Family (2013). Though not a gangster role, one of his finest, subtlest, and most underrated performances was as Louis, the freshly released convict, in Tarantino's Jackie Brown (1997). And of course there is The Irishman (2019), where he plays Frank Sheeran, the man who worked his way up the mob to become Hoffa's bodyguard and then, according to his own confessions, his killer.

The important thing to remember is that seeing as De Niro's filmography now exceeds 100 films, just playing "a gangster" is not really what it's about. De Niro is a star and a character actor, a man who can be a huge box office draw but also make a smaller, character based piece on the side if he wishes to.

The point is, Noodles may be a gangster, but the character is so rounded, multi-dimensional and multi-faceted, that he quickly transcends the mobster mould quite early on. Noodles is a small time hood who would have been happy doing small time crimes for the rest of his life, but the ambitious Max wanted more. When De Niro says he likes the smell of the streets, he confesses to be a product of those streets, a dodgy thief in an expensive suit. He is misplaced among his cronies, misplaced in society, and misplaced in pretty much every place and time he finds himself in. He is the Cagney gangster revived, not the graceful Corleone with a cat on his knee in his plush, polished office. De Niro gives Noodles so much depth that, even as the film ends, he is even more of a labyrinthine maze of contradictions and twists than he was to us at the start.

"God Bless America!"

How much of the film is designed to be a homage to the classic gangster films is up for questioning. Leone loves America, that much is clear, and his shots of the streets, sidewalks and buildings are lovingly handled. Even the corruption seems to be presented to us as an aspect of America that needs to be, if not celebrated, then at least accepted.

Some might say that Sergio had a "romanticised" view of America. While he exposes the greed and corruption within the American structure, Leone never damns it. He takes it as part of the American dream, or he seems to be doing so at least. Though he never uses it in the plot, an Italian like Leone could perhaps relate to the idea of the immigrant who can come and make a success of himself, ala Vito Corleone, if he works hard enough. After all, Leone was in America selling his new film idea for years, working hard to get studio interest and backing for his dream project. The fact he did, and that he attracted the man who many saw as the finest actor of his generation, makes Leone's a success story in itself... at least in some ways.

Some critics have spoken of Sergio's infatuation with the myths of America, both the legendary Wild West and the modern day cowboy, the gangster. To American Film, this theory was raised, to which Leone had his own view. "I am not fascinated, as you say, by the myth of the West, or by the myth of the gangster," he said. "I am not hypnotized, like everyone east of New York and west of Los Angeles, by the mythical notions of America. I'm talking about the individual, and the endless horizon—El Dorado. I believe that cinema, except in some very rare and outstanding cases, has never done much to incorporate these ideas. And if you think about it, America itself has never made much of an effort in that direction either. But there is no doubt that cinema, unlike political democracy, has done what it can. Just consider Easy Rider, Taxi Driver, Scarface, or Rio Bravo. I love the vast spaces of John Ford and the metropolitan claustrophobia of Martin Scorsese, the alternating petals of the American daisy. America speaks like fairies in a fairy tale: 'You desire the unconditional, then your wishes are granted. But in a form you will never recognize.' My moviemaking plays games with these parables. I appreciate sociology all right, but I am still enchanted by fables, especially by their dark side. I think, in any case, that my next film won't be another American fable. But I say that here and I deny it here, too."

As epic as Once Upon a Time in America is, less emphasis is on the history of America itself and more on the individual journeyman making his way through key events and iconic eras. It is, in fact, a fable, one in which the lessons are learned the hard way. In this case, the lone drifter is not The Man With No Name, no poncho clad outlaw, but a heavily flawed man who happens to be a mobster. Leone employs the epic structure to give us an epic character study, a man capable of such lows that it remains a mystery why we still care to see how his tale ends. But in many ways America itself is the heart of the film, beating away in spite of certain blackened areas of rot.

"America is so varied and exciting that after six months, you go back and find it completely changed," Sergio added. "America interests me above all because it is so filled with contradictions, interesting contradictions, which change constantly. Even if you've decided that you don't want to deal with that subject again, before you know it, the desire comes back to do it yet again. The world is in America. In Italy is only Italy. France is full of France. Germany is full of Germany. In a continent that contains the entire world, contradictions are, of course, constantly arising. One of these contradictions that I like... is that two of the biggest moneymaking films in America were Mary Poppins and Deep Throat. One, of course, is the opposite of the other. But most likely seen by the same public. They are alive, these contradictions. And they give vitality and fervour to the nation. But they are nonetheless great contradictions."

Given the fact that Leone opens and closes his film with "God Bless America" (the ghostly revellers sing it as they drive past the aged Noodles just after the garbage truck goes by), it is a celebration through and through. Though he doesn't encourage us to applaud any actual real life violence, he stylises the movie violence in a way to make it accessible, and seem less brutal somehow, more surrealistic and exotic. An Italian through and through, he takes the poetic, European approach to the violence rather than the gritty. Blowing out people's eye balls may sound like the vilest thing you could put on screen, but Leone handles it so artfully as to make it a scene of dark beauty.

Though Leone focuses on the rise of two New York Jews to the top of the crime world, Leone doesn't blame or condemn America itself for allowing men to achieve such stature with the acts they commit. America has it all for the taking, but we as individuals choose the way we will make it, if we decide to try that is. Noodles and Max choose violence, and take all that crooked America can offer them; money, women, power, all achieved by instilling fear in others. They do so arrogantly, and devoid of thought of ramifications and consequences, ignorant to the feelings of others. Does Leone make the gangster a cool, admirable outlaw figure? I have to say no. Noodles and Max are too devoid of morals to be likeable or worthy of any hero worship.

Even though Max and Noodles started from the same roots, the same streets, the same crimes, they end up drastically different. Noodles looks every bit the lonely homeless drifter in the 1968 scenes that he may as well have his pockets turned inside out. He was never ambitious in the way Max was. He was happy to bum along, beating and extorting and robbing on a small scale, always content with enough money at any given time, as long as it fit into his wallet and bulged his pocket. Max on the other hand, had his sights set elsewhere, and when we compare the two men's plights as older men, Max has transformed into the ageing face of cold capitalist greed itself.

Does the film, as some have suggested, serve as a metaphor for the rise of the cruel and calculating idea of capitalism? If so, then Max is the mega rich, and Noodles may well represent the poor worker, the man who tries his best but never comes out on top. Hunched, receding, wrinkly eyed and tired, Noodles drifts around like a spirit in a land he once knew, which he could have owned, but now barely recognises. Max has taken the crown jewels and the throne, and he offers them to Noodles by suggesting he kill him. Does Max offer his life out of guilt? Or does he know he is already a doomed man anyway? Is it because someone else is out to destroy him, or does he sincerely feel remorse for Noodles? It's another mystery. But the case for a capitalist metaphor is not too far a stretch.

Sweet melancholia...

Some of the most powerful moments in Once Upon a Time in America, and indeed in all of Sergio's films, are scenes with no dialogue. Seeing as this film really is an in depth study of one man - albeit a man struggling with another man - through whose eyes we see the passing of time, the unfolding of mysteries and the occurrence of many turbulent events, it's interesting to note it is not a film of flash dialogue. Sure, there are quotable lines throughout, but the dialogue is written as people might have spoken in that time. In truth, in my view at least, the finest moments are when the actors are silent, pensive or in contemplation; when they give a look and a glance; when mood, music and imagery combine to create the true magic. In this respect, he is among the purest of filmmakers.

"The truth is that I am not a director of action, as, in my view, neither was John Ford," Leone told American Film. "I'm more a director of gestures and silences. And an orator of images. However, if you really want it, I'll declare that I agree with old F. Scott Fitzgerald. I often say myself that action is character. But it's true that, to be more precise, I say, Ciack! Action and character, please. Certainly we must mean the same thing. At other times—for example when I'm at the dinner table—I sometimes say, Ciack! Let's eat. Pass the salt."

Perhaps it's just me, but the more melancholic the film gets, the more beautiful it becomes. As Quentin Tarantino noted, it's a credit to Leone that we can come away from such a brutal, at times horrific movie, and speak so openly about its aesthetic perfection. But this effect of staggering beauty is undoubtedly down to all the right elements combining together. There is an ever present sadness throughout, thanks to the endlessly stirring Morricone score, which is ever present, establishing mood and enhancing recurrent themes.

To name favourite scenes from the movie would take me an age. I could list all the best moments, while other fans just as worthy would have their own highlights. But what all these standout scenes have, for me, is the music of Morricone working alongside Leone's camera; and I do feel the balance is right, utterly sublime in fact, whenever Ennio's score couples with Sergio's patient vision.

One scene in particular, which I always tend to think back on, is when Noodles' driver has just driven Deborah away. Noodles, distant from the camera, stands alone on the road with his jacket over his arm. We see a pair of heads go past in the distance, two people cycling together by the sea in the morning air. The heartbreaking music plays and Noodles, alone, staggers off. It's a shot that seems inconsequential, but again, it's these little details which add up. Some directors might not have even put this shot in, but Leone lingers on him walking off for around 30 seconds.

It segues perfectly into the scene of Deborah getting on the train. She buys herself a newspaper and gets on board. As the camera pans up to reveal the busy platform, Deborah takes a window seat. Through the thick smoke emerges Noodles, hands in pockets, looking tired, distant and heartbroken by his own wrong doings. Leone stays on De Niro's face, watching the train until it is out of sight, as the smoke fills the air around him. Noodles walks away, and the camera remains on the beautiful still of the smoke itself. Again, this scene in the hands of another filmmaker may have lasted 20 seconds, but Leone lets it linger for nearly two minutes. The important thing is, he doesn't feel the need to rush off to the next scene. It is this slowness, this sense of patience and savouring every moment, every piece of film, every single frame, that makes the picture such a perversely addictive experience. It is a film where each such moment makes up the whole, where watching scenes or highlights seems to be doing the whole vision an injustice. In modern film, directors are ever so keen to bounce along to the next action scene, the next punch up, the next special effects feast or superhero battle, that they rarely stand still to enjoy something simple and, though considered boring these days, beautiful. It takes a viewing of Once Upon a Time in America to learn that sometimes savouring nothing at all, or very little, is worth more than all the CGI sequences in the world.

An Opium Dream?

Writer Leo Benvenuti tells an interesting story in the documentary Once Upon A Time: Sergio Leone. During one screening of the film, Leone and Benvenuti stood across the street from the theatre and waited for the audience to come out at the end of the movie, so they could see the reactions on their faces, hear their thoughts and views on the film. One man recognised Sergio and approached him. He told him it was a great experience, but went on to quiz the director about the significance of De Niro's manic grin at the end of the film. Leone pointed out to the man that the film starts in an opium den, and ends in one. "So maybe," Leone began. But the man interrupted him. "No, no, please," said the man. Clearly, he did not wish to believe that the film had been one big, long and haunted opium dream.

Though this theory has been discussed over the years, and some have rubbished it, when you re-evaluate the idea, it begins to make some sense. You may not want to believe it, but you certainly have to acknowledge it. If you go to 1933, and the scene where Noodles sees the police take away the bodies of his friends that rainy night, there is only one place he would go straight afterwards - the opium den. It's his only place of escape. He goes there after raping Deborah and watching her leave. Cockeye even suggests that he came to look for Noodles, found him at the den, but he was so whacked out that he didn't even recognise him. He was just saying "Deborah!" deliriously. The opium den was not just a casual hang out for Noodles, but a place where he could get out of his mind, escape reality and forget his problems. The triple whammy death of his three closest friends would surely send him into a drugged out hibernation; and it is here where the nightmare/dream concept comes into place.

If we believe Noodles beds down and starts puffing away into a dreamy hallucinatory world, then he imagines himself as an old man coming home after 35 years in hiding. He sees a changed world, and follows the cryptic clues into finding out the "truth" about Max. The idea that Max planted the tip off idea in Noodles' head (thanks to Carol), then took everything Noodles had held dear (Deborah), living a new life as Bailey, is so far fetched that it really could be a product of a stoned out mind. That Noodles refuses to acknowledge Max/Bailey's tale also suggests that some subconscious corner of Noodles' brain refuses to fully believe this opium daydream.

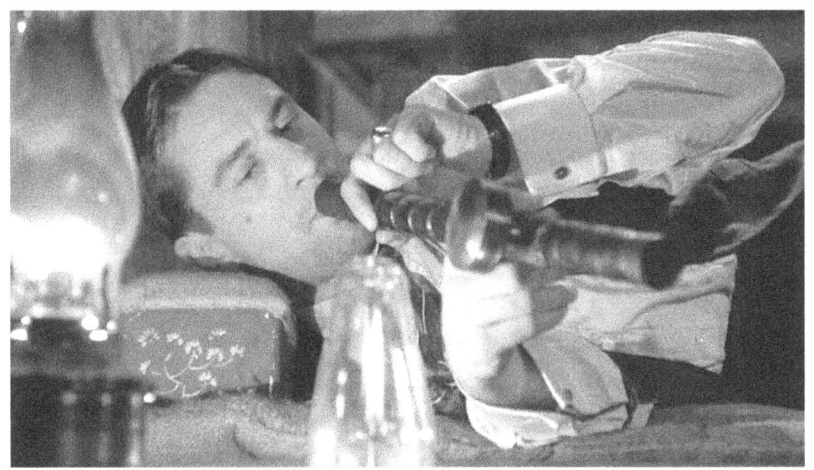

Noodles in the opium den

Noodles also goes back to his childhood, which people often do when contemplating their past and where they went wrong. Everything in these sequences is undoubtedly true, though some of it may be embellished through the passage of time and the haze of opium.

The hideous rape of Deborah is another traumatic experience, along with the demise of his chums, which is enough to push him into a downward, hedonistic spiral of opium and self punishment. In the real world, many people do turn to drink and drugs to forget, to deal with pain, psychological hang ups or horrific incidents which refuse to leave their head. Noodles' smile at the very end of the film shows a man at peace, never happier than when he's lying back with a fresh hit. And this is not the pleasant smile of a man who has found contentment, it's the crinkled grin of a fool, so out of his mind that he can barely do anything but sit there and beam away into another world, like a manic jester, while another bong is loaded up.

If the viewer refuses to believe this theory, then it's only because one has invested so much time, hope and feeling into the 1968 sequences that we desperately wish it to be the real deal. Leone must have thought this was a serious conclusion to tie up any of the loose ends (telling a fan of the film so pretty much clarifies this), but he left it open for the viewer to choose this option or not. Going against this, one sees the film as a long, majestic look through the past. It's either the tale of a man regretting his whole journey, or a man escaping his errors through a mind warping substance. Either way, there is really no happy ending for Noodles, the bitter old man or the beaten up waster.

Taste of Cinema was just one of the publications to support the dream idea. "It is, at times, an incredibly ambiguous story," they wrote in 2014. "For years, the idea of the 'dream theory' has floated around in regards to how one interprets Once Upon A Time in America. Think of the first and last time we meet Noodles in this story, the exact location. We meet him in an opium den. This is a gorgeous illustration of the idea of the 'unreliable narrator' or the fact that we see the story from the perspective of a blown mind. The 'dream theory' goes as thus. Everything until the death of Max, Patsy and Cockeye is real, as is the pursuit of gangsters from 'The Combination' looking for Noodles and slaying or beating anyone who dares to get in their way. However, the latter day scenes in the film, set in 1968, may not in actual fact be reality and could be nothing more than an opium dream Noodles is having. The surprising scene, such as when Noodles meets Deborah's son, David, manage to be both plausible and exaggerated at the same time. Ditto the story arc involving Bailey. However, at the same time, one notices details that are dead on to that part of the era, such as the cars, television and hippies in the background on one shot set in a train station. Personally, I can see evidence for both interpretations. However, I just like to let that train of thought and interpretation hang there and be ambiguous."

Do I really believe it's an opium dream? Well, as I am sure is the case with many fans of the film, it depends on how I am feeling. The bitter Noodles in his later years is a such a sad figure that I almost *want* to believe it's all an illusion. But then again, he was such a questionable man in his younger years anyway, that maybe the life of a drifting, lonely old ghost is all he deserves after what he has done. But this mystery keeps the film alive; it keeps the cult strong and the theories coming along thickly. It's the same with the enigmatic disappearance of Max. Did he really go into the back of the garbage truck? Did he throw something else in and then disappear out of sight? If he did or didn't is irrelevant. As James Woods later put it, "Either way, he ain't showing up to the Red Sox game next Tuesday."

The mysteries and unexplained elements of Once Upon a Time in America are what make it the enigmatic masterpiece it is; explain them and the puzzle is solved. They separate the movie from all the other, more straight forward gangster films out there. So let's keep guessing, and may we never know the truth... whatever that is.

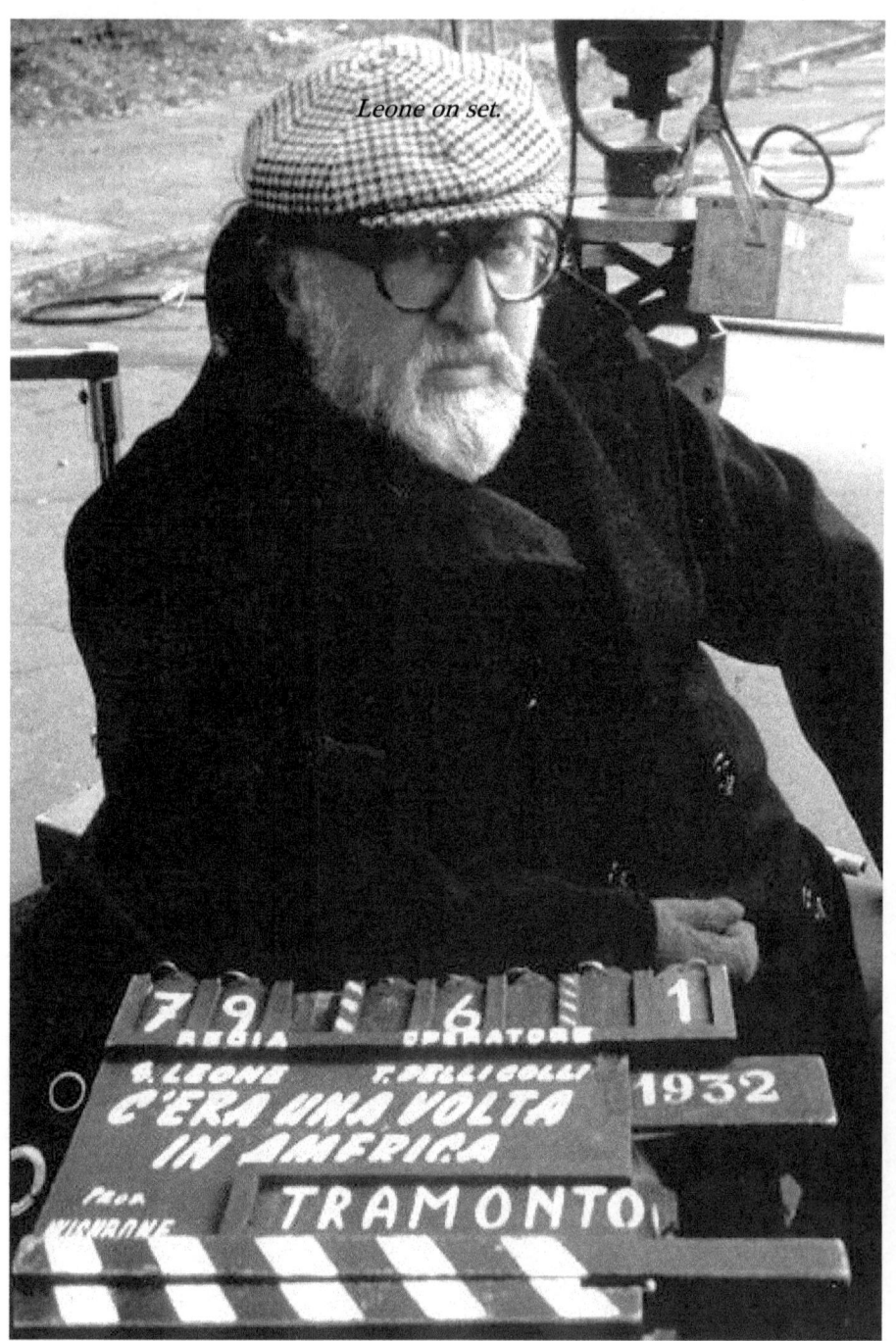
Leone on set.

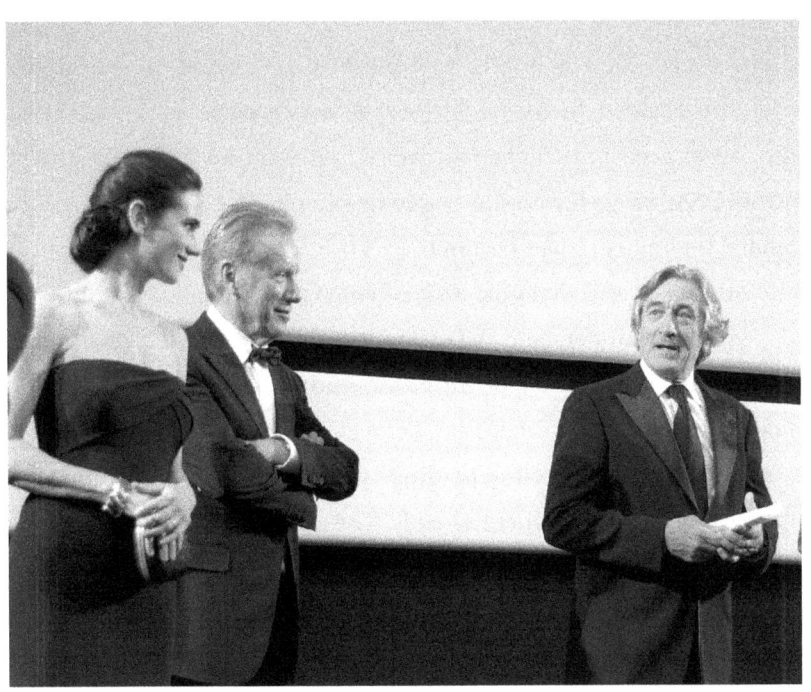

REACTION AND LEGACY

"Once Upon a Time in America is my best film, bar none - I swear - and I knew that it would be from the moment I got Harry Gray's book in my hand. I'm glad I made it, even though during the filming I was as tense as Dick Tracy's jaw. It always goes like that. Shooting a film is awful, but to have made a movie is delicious."
- Sergio Leone, 1984

Once Upon a Time in America is unique in the film world for a number of reasons. Artistically, it's one of the most sweeping, grand and ambitious films from the 1980s (the blockbuster generation it so stood out from), but it was treated with an almost sickening amount of disrespect when it finally was finished. Its release is one of the most complicated in movie history. A masterpiece by a master of film, it was accepted all over the world, but received unfair treatment in the USA, its victimisation a good example of how commercially minded the industry had become.

If you look at the changing face of cinema in the late 70s and early 80s, you can understand why the movie found itself in limbo. Consider the blockbuster boom of the mid to late seventies. In 1976, personal, gritty films like Taxi Driver and even Rocky were high earners. They were intelligent films, focusing on the underdog, the anti hero who goes against the odds. The success of the former is the most extraordinary when you consider that in today's market, it would be classed as a low budget art house flick and probably not even grace the big screen. Only a year later, the industry was revolutionised by the arrival of George Lucas' Star Wars, which woke studios up to the box office potential of exciting adventure films. It also kick-started an industry of merchandising and tie ins; lunch boxes, figures, quilt covers... you name it. The merch often outsold the film.

As the 1980s went on, this mentality had only heightened. If it didn't have a cute and cuddly alien in it, or a wise cracking robot, then your film wasn't going to cut it in the bigger arena. A four hour gangster epic with a jumbled up plot, spanning fifty years, cutting back and forth from one era to another, featuring graphic violence and disturbing rape scenes, didn't really stand a chance in a time when Indiana Jones and Beverly Hills Cop were filling the theatres. I am not going to say that all "blockbusters" are empty headed, because that's film snobbery and simply untrue. A look at some of the other hits of 1984, the year Leone's film came out, gives us mainstream gems like Gremlins and Ghostbusters. (De Niro himself was with Meryl Streep in Falling in Love, an overlooked romantic drama, while Woods enjoyed success in the hit thriller, Against All Odds.) Though some of the bigger films are good fun, they are not remotely challenging. As the studios were now telling us (and, it has to be said, how they were engineering it), audiences didn't want a challenge. They wanted a massive bucket of popcorn, a fizzy drink and two hours of daft escapism. The sprawling tale of Noodles and Max wasn't exactly the biggest draw of 1984. This drew a line between what was serious art, and what was merely product. There was, and is, a place for both, but separating the two is essential in understanding the business aspects of the movies.

The film received acclaim at Cannes in 84, where the lucky viewers got to enjoy Sergio's vision on the big screen. One notable person present at the screening was Roger Ebert, who wrote, "Is the film too long? Yes and no. Yes, in the sense that it takes real concentration to understand Leone's story construction, in which everything may or may not be an opium dream, a nightmare, a memory, or a flashback, and that we have to keep track of characters and relationships over fifty years. No, in the sense that the movie is compulsively and continuously watchable and that the audience did not stir or grow restless as the epic unfolded."

Such is the mystery of this film. At 3 hours long and 40 minutes (4 hours 20 if you are watching the recently unleashed Extended Cut on Blu Ray), it is unquestionably a sprawling epic, but really only feels like half that running time; which is odd, as it moves slowly with grace. Though there are action sequences mixed in (shoot outs, fights, robberies etc.), it's never a film which rushes itself to conclusions. In fact, it takes its time, and we the viewer go with Noodles at his pace. It's like spending time with an old man, who might be telling you the winding tale of his life. Whether you believe him or not is up to you. Today, it's hard to understand that such a film, by such a director, would be treated so shabbily.

The Cannes cut did make the rounds in European cinemas, but unbelievably, Warners sliced the film right down to 2 hours and 20 minutes for its US release. Placing events in chronological order, rather than in the disjointed form Leone rightly intended, the film lost all its power, dreaminess and singularity. What remained was a by-the-numbers gangster story, starting with childhood, racing through the adult years and ending up in 1968 with Noodles as an old man looking back. This conventional structure took all the mystique from the movie. Anybody who had seen both cuts could not help but point out how bad the shorter version was, even stars of the movie itself!

"Well, visually I was blown away," Julie Cohen told me recently, looking back on the first time she saw the studio's butchered cut of the movie. "Seeing all the pieces come together - performances, locations, cinematography (Tonino) and the music (Morricone) was pure poetry and all the elements were there, but... the first time I saw the movie it was the edited version released by the studio. The story was just not clear. I was disappointed by how much was missing and how hard it was to figure out what was going on. Trying to tell the story in chronological order made it more mundane and took away its dreamy magic somehow. I was also surprised by some of the violence, especially towards women. Those scenes were difficult to watch. So brutal and realistic. But it is a story about brutal men, crime and guilt. Responsibility, loyalty, greed... that's heavy stuff. Now that it's been restored to Sergio's vision and now that we know it was his final film, it has so much more resonance and power. Now when you watch it it's like an opera full of pain, love, loss, regret. I mean it's BIG and mythic! The performances really hold up, James Woods, Tuesday Weld - these are great performances. And the flashback scenes are so sweet to me now. We were all really young kids doing brave and difficult work. I'm so proud of the work we did and I'm so grateful to have been a part of it."

Other cast members were outraged by the savage cuts. "I hope they burn the fucking negative!" James Woods was quoted as saying upon seeing the Hollywood edit. "Three weeks before the film is released, they have the assistant editor of Police Academy chop it to fucking ribbons! I mean, do you think I was suicidal? The film got fucking slaughtered by the critics, as well it should have. It was fucking dead in the water."

Critical reaction to the 139 minute version was often very harsh. Pauline Kael had rubbished it mercilessly, but then wrote a positive piece on Leone's fuller version. Though she still had some issues, she praised De Niro's work. "In its full length, the movie has a tidal pull back toward the earliest memories, and an elegiac tone. Partly, I think, this is the result of De Niro's measured performance. He makes you feel the weight of Noodles' early experiences and his disappointment in himself. He makes you feel that Noodles never forgets the past, and it's his all-encompassing guilt that holds the film's different sections together. De Niro was offered his choice of the two leading roles—Max, the go-getter, the tricky, hothead boss of the group, and the watchful, indecisive Noodles, the loser, who spends the years from 1921 to 1933 in prison. I respect De Niro's decision, because he may have thought that the passive Noodles, whose urges explode in bursts of aggression against women, would be a reach, would test him. James Woods, who plays Max, dominated the short version; he actually provided its brighter moments... In the full version, De Niro gives the film its dimensions. He keeps a tiny flame alive in his eyes, and his performance builds."

Kael had issues, as others did too, with McGovern's work, feeling, rather understandably (though I disagree) that she doesn't quite live up to the "one great love" she is in the eyes of Noodles. "And although Deborah, the dancer-actress that Noodles loves all his life, is marvellously vivid in her young girlhood, when she's played by Jennifer Connelly (who's so clear-eyed she walks away with the twenties passages), the role of the adult Deborah is taken over by Elizabeth McGovern, who's classically miscast," Kael complained. "McGovern's inability to live up to the idea that she's De Niro's great love weakens the film's showpiece romantic sequence, set in a vast Art Deco oceanfront restaurant on Long Island—a restaurant that is closed for the season but that Noodles has rented for the evening, with a full staff and a dance orchestra. The scene is meant to reveal Noodles' yearning nature; it's clear that Leone was thinking about Gatsby and lost dreams."

I feel Kael, as great as she often was, was dead wrong on this point. But she was not alone. The New York Times were openly harsh towards the film too, but I honestly feel they didn't actually grasp what was going on. "Sergio Leone," wrote Vincent Canby, "the Italian director who gave class to the term 'spaghetti western,' has made some weird movies in his day but nothing to match Once Upon a Time in America, a lazily hallucinatory epic that means to encapsulate approximately 50 years of American social history into a single film. Like most films that have been so clumsily abbreviated, this shorter version of Once Upon a Time in America seems endless, possibly because whatever internal structure it might have had no longer exists. It's a collection of occasionally vivid but mostly unfathomable incidents in which people are introduced and then disappear with the unexplained suddenness of victims of mob murders. Mr. De Niro and Mr. Woods might well be giving good performances, but it's impossible to tell from the evidence being shown here. At one point, the story appears to require that each assumes the other's character. Nothing in the movie looks quite the way it should. Hilarious anachronisms abound, as might be expected in a production that was shot in Rome, Montreal and New York. When Deborah leaves for Hollywood from Grand Central, the terminal looks like Rome's and the 20th Century Limited like the Orient Express. Once Upon a Time in America, which is not to be confused with Mr. Leone's far wiser Once Upon a Time in the West (1969), opens today at the Beekman and other theaters."

As the years passed by, the film started to gain a bit of a following. Those who respected Leone's vision enjoyed his fuller, meatier cut, and the characters of Noodles and Max slowly began to enter the canon of classic movie gangsters. Though it still befuddled some viewers, the film won enough over to get its own cult. But one can see why some folk, particularly blockbuster minded people, might be instantly dismissive of it.

On a personal level, I was transfixed from the first time I saw it, from the very first scene in fact. It was a film I had read about and was desperate to see. In the pre-internet days though, finding a film that was out of print wasn't easy. If it wasn't in HMV, Virgin or Choices video, then the chances were slim. For me, TV was my way in. I recall my sister recording it for me in the 90s. She and her partner had Sky TV and I didn't. So I went over with a video and left it there for them to tape the movie. I recall that they did try to watch it, but were put off by the "annoying phone ringing" in the opening section. Hardly film buffs, they obviously found it too much for their TV fed brains. They turned off the television and got on with doing something else instead.

I got the tape home and excitedly sat down to enjoy this "two hour" gangster film, only for it to end abruptly with the caption: "part two will be on next week." Desperately I called them back and told them part two needed recording that Friday night. They were not pleased! But I was pleased once part two was in my possession. The film instantly cast a spell over me, and I became addicted to watching it. I devoured every minute, tried to make sense of its twists and turns, though parts did baffle my teenage mind. Sometimes I would just put it on while going about my day, stopping to watch certain bits, absorb the atmosphere, the mood and the music while doing other things. These days I watch it quite regularly; I simply let the beauty of it wash over me. It's become an experience rather than the mere viewing of a film.

Obviously though, I was not and am not alone, for it has many dedicated followers. That said, in the days before the internet, where people can connect and relate over their loves and obsessions, being a fan of Once Upon a Time in America was a lonely experience. I often felt like the only one who knew about this wonderful movie. Then its cult began to grow. Thanks to its DVD release, its reputation deepened and its influence seemed to expand. Quite soon, people were mentioning it in the same breath as The Godfather. Some even claimed it to be a superior film.

Things got truly exciting for the more devoted fans of the film in 2012, when Martin Scorsese led the way in getting the full version restored and seen widely. Assembling every bit of footage they could, and cleaning it up lovingly, it was soon possible that a 251 minute version could be presented at Cannes, 28 years after the film was originally released. De Niro, Woods, McGovern, Connelly, Morricone and others attended the screening. As expected, reaction to both the film and the gathered talent was truly blistering.

Speaking from the stage before the screening, De Niro, standing alongside McGovern, Woods and Connelly, held the microphone and said:

"Good evening everybody. I am so pleased to be here tonight to present this new edition of Once Upon a Time in America. Standing here with my fellow actors, Jimmy Woods, Elizabeth McGovern, Jennifer Connelly, the composer Ennio Morricone... it brings back the experience of working with the great Sergio Leone. I have such fond memories of working with Sergio, as we all do. I remember it was one of the longest movies I ever worked on. I don't think Sergio ever wanted to finish it. I worked on it for about a year."

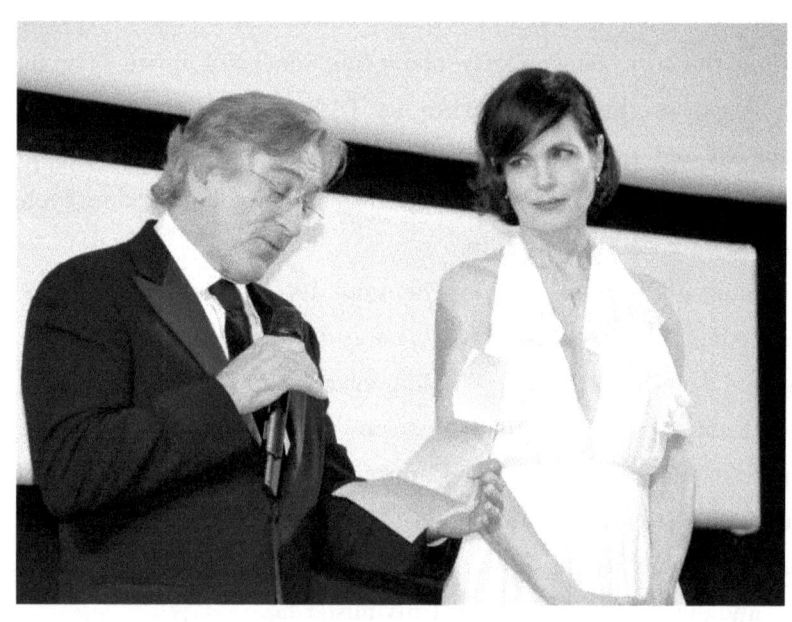

De Niro and McGovern at the 2012 Cannes premier of the full length Once Upon a Time in America

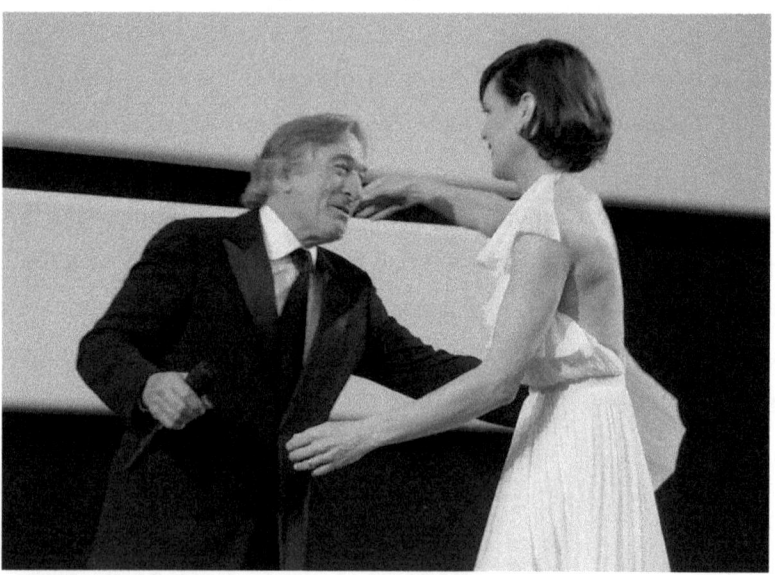

Passing the microphone to James Woods, the man who the audience would soon be seeing as Max addressed them with passion:

"It was first time in my life and the only time ever since, that we (the cast) bonded like a family. This is a very important night because Sergio Leone, his love for his cast and technicians made it possible for this once in a lifetime experience. And now, finally for you, this great vision of Sergio Leone..."

Though the cut went down well, this version didn't make it to a wider cinema release across the world, and screenings were delayed time and again, especially when the film was supposed to make its way to the UK. Despite complications, since then, Once Upon a Time in America has seen another revival of interest. DVD releases have included restored scenes, and the extended 251 minute cut is even out on Blu Ray. Retrospective reviews are nearly always glowing. Major pieces have been written on the movie and it has now been put up there as a true cinematic classic.

The New York Post, excited about its upcoming theatrical screening, wrote of the extended cut that it was worth "every second... Sometimes even a masterpiece can get better — as audiences at the New York Film Festival will discover when a new, extended restoration of Sergio Leone's enigmatic gangster epic Once Upon a Time in America makes its American debut Saturday. While the longer version that's circulated for the last 30 years is brilliantly crafted — it's one of my favourites from the era — there's always been a sense that pieces are missing. Longer isn't always better: Heaven's Gate, another epic flop of the era that was drastically cut and later restored, remains an incoherent, self-indulgent bore. But adding 22 minutes to Once Upon a Time in America only enhances Leone's brilliant saga of guilt and betrayal."

Boston Phoenix hailed the film, writing, "Another director might have turned the same material into a rags-to-riches-to-rags story. Leone transcends clichés through reverie and metaphor, and through a layering of the action that treats the story's several eras like double and triple exposures. There are moments in this movie so breathtakingly daring, so grand, that they're romantically transcendent."

Starburst wrote of the extended blu-ray: "If you let this film envelope you, let it become a companion for a few hours, it will deliver an experience you will not find from many sources. By the end you will have developed a lasting relationship with Noodles and Max, an understanding of their motivations and an insight into their world. If you already own a copy of America you may not need this in your collection. If you don't, buy it now and set aside a Saturday night for a little cinematic indulgence."

Esquire wrote a fabulous glowing piece on the film in 2018.: "Told in a kaleidoscope of unchronological fragments, the film presents the emotional passage of these two men, Noodles and Max, as they recklessly tear their way through an unmerciful society of systemic oppression and cruelty. It is smarter, superiorly affecting, more artfully shot, edited, and scored than any film of its ilk—a bonafide champion of the form, tragically overlooked in our culture. Somehow, in spite of all their deplorable actions, it's just impossible to take your eyes off the criminals of Leone's "Kosher Nostra" film. Like the characters of all the truly great mob classics, Noodles and Max are empowered as a by product of their environment: early 20th century America. In typical Leone fashion, the film studies the faces of its cast intimately and defiantly, preferring long, extreme close-ups over action or set pieces to convey emotional depth. These close ups have become quintessential touchstones in the dictionaries of cinema, with filmmakers like Quentin Tarantino expressing publicly the deep importance of the Leone close up."

Fans of the film are now very lucky, given that we can see restored scenes that were cut from the original. They are still a little grainy of course, but their shadiness adds to the sheer excitement of watching another few minutes of Noodles in his journey to unravelling the mysteries of his life. Though adding little to the plot, they do, if anything, make the whole thing even more enigmatic.

One memorable scene involves Noodles visiting the funeral home to arrange burial plans for his "friend", featuring Louise Fletcher (who famously played Nurse Ratched in One Flew Over the Cuckoo's Nest) as the funeral director. It's a great, moody scene, and its mystique is infectious viewing. As De Niro and Fletcher chat, he notices a car has been following him around, the faceless driver watching his every move. Noodles takes down the license plate. It's a fabulous little sequence, and really should have been put in the picture in the first place.

Another moment which has recently been restored is a scene right after Noodles drives the car into the water following the shoot out involving Burt Young. It shows the boys frolicking and laughing together in the water, segueing into a sequence where Noodles slowly drifts past diggers and watches the car that had been following him earlier explode into pieces. It's so unsettlingly powerful that one can understand why it pained Leone so much to trim down such beautifully filmed scenes to please the studio.

There is also a fabulous scene involving Deborah, seen on stage performing in her white make up. Although it's nicely staged and directed, it might have taken the edge off Noodles seeing her in the dressing room for the first time. A similar point could be made of the cut scene involving Woods and Treat Williams, with the latter as an aged Conwy. The scene is nicely played, but again, it takes the impact away from Max/Bailey's reunion with Noodles; and of course that beautiful shot of when Max walks to the window, before the camera, to gaze outside.

But the excitement generated by these sequences, and the reactions of long time fans, highlights what a serious piece of work Leone's film is. It has stood the test of time, no doubt about it, and only gets stronger, more poignant, more moving and more devastatingly beautiful as time goes by. It's become the filmmaker's favourite film, something many directors hold up as a kind of zenith. In recent years it's been finding its way on to seminal critics' lists; Sight and Sound's writers placed it the tenth greatest film of all time, while Time Out had it at number 9 in their Top 50 gangster films. It encourages debate, theorising, film geekery, even obsession. It's self contained, has no sequels, no spin offs, and even its tragic butchering adds something to its cult of appeal. I honestly feel that as the years go by its reputation will only grow more.

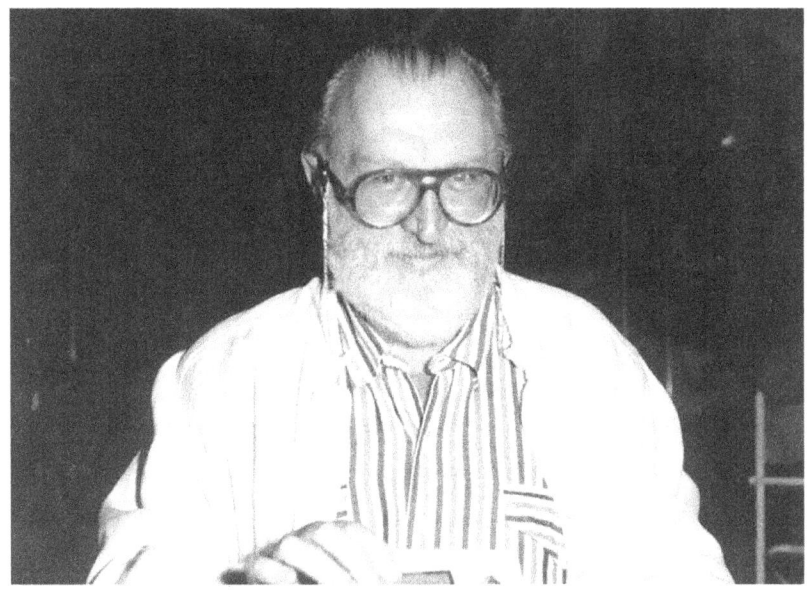
Sergio Leone in 1987, two years before his death

For Leone, his dream film inevitably turned out to be his last. In 1989 he died of a heart attack at the age of only 60. He had been planning a new movie, Siege of Leningrad, but it was not to be. Two years before his death, he gave an interview where he expressed his worries about modern filmmaking, and its future as an art form. Once Upon a Time in America, by then only three years old, was already looking like a thing of the distant past, especially when comparing it to the faster rhythms of the modern blockbusters. "I'm terrified by young people who are doing what they think is filmmaking," Leone said, sounding disenchanted with his beloved medium. "What they're really doing is taking that convulsed, fast rhythm of commercials. It's not filmmaking. I've seen films that have made as much as $100, $200 million, but they're not films. They're images. They're flashes. They're many beautiful images, lots of things to look at. They capture you. But it's not a film. It's not something that involves you in a story. They go to cinema now to be blown away by the effects. Just like you would if you would walk into a discothèque or any place else, with noise and lights. Because they need to get away for one or two hours. So they go, but nothing remains inside of them."

The saddest part is that Leone didn't even live long enough to see his great masterpiece gain the credit and acclaim it always deserved. If he could be here now to see the Blu Ray and DVD editions of his film, learn about the 2012 Cannes unveiling of the full cut, read the reviews, notices and praise heaped upon it, then he would be a very happy man indeed. Heartbroken he may have been by the shabby treatment of Once Upon a Time in America, Leone can rest assured, wherever he may be, that his film is now a classic; and to some, the finest picture ever made.

ONCE UPON A TIME IN AMERICA CREDITS

CAST

Robert De Niro - David "Noodles" Aaronson

James Woods - Max

Elizabeth McGovern - Deborah

Treat Williams - Jimmy O'Donnell

Tuesday Weld - Carol

Burt Young - Joe

Joe Pesci - Frankie Monaldi

Danny Aiello - Police Chief Aiello

William Forsythe - Cockeye

James P. Hayden - Patsy

Darlanne Fluegel - Eve

Larry Rapp - Fat Moe

Amy Ryder - Peggy

Scott Tiler - Young Noodles

Rusty Jacobs - David, Max's son

Rusty Jacobs - Young Max

Jennifer Connelly - Young Deborah

Adrian Curran - Young Cockeye

Brian Bloom - Young Patsy

Julie Cohen - Young Peggy

Noah Moazezi - Dominic

James Russo - Bugsy

Karen Shallo - Mrs. Aiello

Richard Foronjy - Whitey

Sergio Leone - Ticket Agent

Mort Freeman - Scott Coffey

Linda Ipanema - Nurse Thompson

Dutch Miller - Van Linden

Robert Harper - Sharkey

Richard Bright - Chicken Joe

Gerard Murphy - Crowning

Olga Karlatos - Woman in the Puppet Theater

Mario Brega - Mandy

Ray Dittrich - Trigger

Frank Gio - Beefy

Angelo Florio - Willie the Ape

Clem Caserta - Al Capuano

Jerry Strivelli - Johnny Capuano

Marvin Scott - Interviewer

Paul Herman - Monkey

Joey Faye - Adorable Old Man

Richard Zobel - Reporter

Baxter Harris - Reporter

Arnon Milchan - Chauffeur

Bruno Iannone - Thug

Marcia Jean Kurtz - Max's Mother

Estelle Harris - Peggy's Mother

Cliff Cudney - Mounted Policeman

Paul Farentino - 2nd Mounted Policeman

CREW

Sergio Leone - Director, Screenwriter

Arnon Milchan - Producer

Claudio Mancini - Executive Producer

Fred Caruso - Executive Producer

Benito Stefanelli - Stunts

Carlo Simi - Art Director

Cis Corman - Casting

Dennis Benatar - First Assistant Director

Ennio Morricone - Composer (Music Score)

Enrico Medioli - Screenwriter

Franco Arcalli - Screenwriter

Franco Ferrini - Screenwriter

Gabriella Pescucci - Costume Designer

Gil Rossellini - Production Assistant

Giovanni Corridori - Special Effects

Giovanni Natalucci - Set Designer

Gretchen Rau - Set Designer

Harry Grey - Book Author

James T. Singelis - Art Director

Joy Todd - Casting

Leo Benvenuti - Screenwriter

Manilo Rocchetti - Makeup

Mario Cotone Supervisor/Manager

Nilo Jacoponi - Makeup

Nino Baragli - Editor

Piero De Bernardi - Screenwriter

Robert Benmussa - Consultant/advisor

Stuart Kaminsky - Dialogue Writer

Tonino Delli Colli - Cinematographer

Walter Massi - Production Designer

References and Ackowledgements

I would like to say a special thanks to James Woods, who has been extremely supportive during various projects as of late, especially this very book. I also wish to thank Robert Harper, Amy Wells, Renato Cesaro, Steve Kirshoff and Julie Cohen for sharing their memories of Leone and the film with me. These interviews contributed greatly to the book and I am eternally grateful.

The following articles were useful in completing this book;

Sergio Leone Interview by Marlaine Glicksman
Sergio Leone Interview, American Film
James Woods Interview, Den Of Geek
Empire Magazine, Essay on Once Upon A Time in America
Elizabeth McGovern: De Niro and Me, the Independent
Boston Pheonix, film review
Irish Times, film review
New York Times, film review
The New Yorker, film review
Roger Ebert on Once Upon A Time in America
13 Facts About Once Upon A Time in America

Documentaries and footage;

Once Upon A Time: Sergio Leone
Robert De Niro On Once Upon A Time In America
Cannes 2012 Reunion Video Footage

Sergio Leone: The Way I See Things, Documentary

Books;

Robert De Niro: Movie Top Ten
De Niro by Partick Agan
The Cinema of Robert De Niro by James Cameron Wilson
Sergio Leone, by Christopher Frayling
The Films of Robert De Niro, Douglas Brode
Once Upon A Time in America, Adrian Martin
Hoods, Harry Grey

Picture Credits;

Shutterstock
Dreamstime
Commons
Screenshot of Once Upon a Time in America
copyright of Warner Bros.

ABOUT CHRIS WADE

Chris Wade is a UK based writer, filmmaker and musician. As well as running the acclaimed music project Dodson and Fogg, he has written books on Picasso, Federico Fellini, Marcello Mastroianni and many others. He has also released audiobooks of his comedic fiction, such as Cutey and the Sofaguard, narrated by Rik Mayall. His other projects include Hound Dawg Magazine and Scenes: The Cult and Classic Film Publication. His art films include The Apple Picker (winning Best Film at the Sydney World Film Festival, and featuring Toyah Willcox and Nigel Planer), and he's made documentaries on George Melly, Lindsay Anderson, Charlie Chaplin and Orson Welles.

More info at his website: wisdomtwinsbooks.weebly.com

01858 466131

Order No G57517

ord Day 14 March

① Technical Guidelines
② 3rd Party Cyber.
③ Directors Plan.
   Strategic Integration.

① GE
② Turnerlce
③ Severn Drives.
④ Schneider.

Lightning Source UK Ltd.
Milton Keynes UK
UKHW020640240222
399180UK00009B/604